The Credit Cleanup Book

The Credit Cleanup Book

Improving Your Credit Score, Your Greatest Financial Asset

Shindy Chen

 PRAEGER

AN IMPRINT OF ABC-CLIO, LLC
Santa Barbara, California • Denver, Colorado • Oxford, England

Copyright © 2014 by Shindy Chen

Library of Congress Cataloging-in-Publication Data

Chen, Shindy.
  The credit cleanup book : improving your credit score, your greatest financial asset / Shindy Chen.
     pages cm
  Includes bibliographical references and index.
  ISBN 978-1-4408-3182-9 (hardcopy : alk. paper) — ISBN 978-1-4408-3183-6 (ebook)
1. Credit ratings—United States.   2. Consumer credit—United States.   3. Finance, Personal—United States.   I. Title.
  HG3751.7.C44 2014
  332.7′5—dc23   2014021684

ISBN: 978-1-4408-3182-9
EISBN: 978-1-4408-3183-6

18 17 16 15 14   1 2 3 4 5

This book is also available on the World Wide Web as an eBook.
Visit www.abc-clio.com for details.

Praeger
An Imprint of ABC-CLIO, LLC

ABC-CLIO, LLC
130 Cremona Drive, P.O. Box 1911
Santa Barbara, California 93116–1911

This book is printed on acid-free paper ∞

Manufactured in the United States of America

To my parents. Your hard work paved the way.

To Mary. You continue to inspire me!

A percentage of author royalties will go to non-profit Multiple Sclerosis support organizations.

Contents

Preface

Throughout my financial services career, I discovered that the *only* factor that matters in the journey to home ownership is—I'm sad to say—the credit score.

Many lenders and service providers today continue to use your credit report and score as the sole basis to determine your eligibility for *their* products and services.

From a young age, I started in mortgage loan origination in early 2002, working for nearly a decade in the growing metro Atlanta area. I cut my teeth at a small mortgage brokerage, mastered the basics and processes, and then went on to originate with one of the nation's largest home builders, where I learned most of what I know about originating and credit.

Before ending my career to pursue business school full time, I was leading a regional team at one of the nation's largest banks (which eventually filed bankruptcy during the credit crisis and was later bought by a larger bank). Throughout, I ended up closing upward of 300 mortgage loans, totaling over $100 million in loan volume. During this time I also reviewed hundreds of credit reports and helped coach those borrowers with less-than-perfect credit on how to improve their situations to eventually become mortgage-ready.

My timing was pretty sweet—after all, this was during the housing boom. But by 2008, the economy was dismantled by the credit crisis and the subprime mortgages that fueled the fire. I speak more on my personal experience with subprime mortgages in Chapter 8, "Credit and Your Life."

Nonetheless I recall the large amount of prospective homebuyers that lenders in my region were able to equip with financing. I hope that many are secure in their assets today, despite metro Atlanta being one of the hardest hit by the recession. My clients were first-timers, move-up buyers, investors, those building custom homes—they were also single professionals, independent men and women, young families, older families and empty nesters, and I appreciated more than anything that they trusted me to help realize their home ownership dreams. I can probably recall every face and name.

This was Bush administration-era easy money. Interest rates on home loans were at their lowest in decades. One-hundred-percent home financing was fairly easy to secure, and mortgages with low introductory rates, which could (and did) adjust higher were boldly advertised. This made payments affordable, initially—until they weren't. My own first home was purchased in 2003 with 100 percent financing, at a rate of six percent for only two years, also known as a two-year adjustable rate mortgage (ARM).

I, like many others with an ARM, would eventually rely on my credit, income, and most importantly, my home's appreciation, to successfully refinance at a later date—a viable option for me at the time, but not for many after the bubble burst. The market just lost steam. Housing values stalled, borrowers began to miss payments when rates adjusted higher, and they were stuck with zero refinance options. Like a stack of dominoes, suddenly hundreds of millions in mortgage loans went into default. Many homeowners lost their homes to foreclosure. Lenders closed shop, and the economy spiraled downward.

Here's some perspective: the home builder for which I worked, a former Fortune 250 company called Centex, was eventually purchased by its competitor, Pulte Homes. The bank where I worked, then the nation's fourth largest, Wachovia, filed bankruptcy a month after I left. It was eventually acquired by Wells Fargo (whose mortgage company is now the nation's largest home loan funder by volume).[1]

As of this writing in early 2014, banks are still paying or settling up for unsavory practices related to the risky subprime mortgages they (or the companies they acquired) packaged and sold. In late March, the *Financial Times* reported that Bank of America finally settled for $9.5 billion with the Federal Housing Finance Agency, for its stepchildren's (Countrywide and Merrill Lynch) bad behavior during the subprime boom. The FT reported the bank could end up paying almost $17 billion including Department of Justice (DoJ) payouts after all is said and done.[2] Another major bank, JP Morgan Chase, paid out almost $13 billion in settlements with the DoJ.

Six years on, and our nation's economic health is slowly recovering to prerecessionary conditions. And despite housing strength being a key indicator of economic health, our largest banks are continuing to revise and tighten their lending criteria for home purchases and refinances. So what does that mean for consumers and homeowners?

I'm no longer an originator, but I felt that you, as a consumer in the general public, should know about how your credit report is perceived anytime you apply for services or ask to borrow money. I've since gone on to write and edit content that covers finance and serves financial services professionals, in addition to the creative, technology, and travel industries.

Many former colleagues, credit industry vets and professionals, who are actively working in the credit industry today, were instrumental to sharing their resources, advice, and insights for this book. They are the ones in the field working with and reviewing credit daily, with their eyes and ears to the street, and who know of the changes upon us in this new postrecessionary environment. I've also spoken to some incredibly talented companies and leaders today who, through technology, are building some innovative methods to help people be in control of their money, finances, and ultimately, credit.

We live in vastly different economic times than six years ago, and if you're wondering where to start and what to do regarding understanding, improving, and maintaining a good credit score and error-free credit report, this book is for you.

If you're wondering how you should manage credit card debt or outstanding collections and other derogatory credit information, this book will help.

If you have excellent credit and you're planning on your next big life purchase such as a new car or home, this book will help you determine what matters to lenders in your overall financial picture, such as your income, savings, and debts.

Please use this book the best way you see fit. I stick by and have personally implemented most of the tips myself. I hope that it can be your go-to, primary credit resource, perhaps the only one you'll ever need to understand credit basics.

To you and *your* greatest financial asset,
Shindy Chen

Acknowledgments

I started this project in 2008, after I left the mortgage industry to pursue business school and subsequently combine my love for journalism and media with my finance knowledge. Forget the "left or right brain" debate; I love to write, I love art and design, all things digital and tech, and also numbers and analytics. And I love people who can see that in me and support that.

Many thanks to Beverly Langford for not batting an eyelash when asked for advice on getting published; it's because of great teachers, leaders, and communicators like you, who instill confidence in writers like me. By the way, Beverly's book, *The Etiquette Edge: The Unspoken Rules for Business Success*, is a reminder for anyone, whether self-employed, or working at a start-up or large corporation, that courtesy and manners go a *long* way in business relationships.

Thanks to Stan Wakefield for ever-amusing commentary and giving me the proverbial "kick-in-the-arse" to resume this project upon my return from across the pond. Though the postrecession timing worked out better in the end, don't you think?

Many thanks to Hilary Claggett at ABC-CLIO/Praeger for advice, responsiveness, and insight from start to finish. And for believing in and supporting this project. I doubt many authors have such an experienced editor as you, and I consider myself a lucky one! Also thanks to Nicole Azze, Erin Henry, Catherine Lafuente, and Anthony Chiffolo at ABC-CLIO.

To my friends who also happened to be contributors to this book: the *man* James Dorcely, the inimitable Michael Karp, my dear colleague Joe

Petriccione, the wonderful Jason "sign the f-ing thing" Womack, and the lovely Mary Joan Cunningham. Thank you. I am blessed to have such incredible, smart, and successful people in my personal as well as professional circle.

Many thanks to Chris Welker at Welker and Associates, and Steve White at American Credit Repair, for your willingness to share your expertise—I'm so grateful to you both. To Josh Reich and Krista Berlincourt at Simple, I wish you guys all the best of luck—you are revolutionizing American banking as we know it. To Olivier Lemaignen and Jenn Jacobsen at Credit Sesame for your participation—love what you guys do and thank you. To Bethy Hardeman at Credit Karma, many thanks for your eagerness to help. To Anthony Sprauve at myFICO.com, thanks for your contributions.

To Dana Neal, many thanks for writing the tome on credit and allowing me to share your expertise with the world.

Thank you to Jeff Kuns, for being patient while showing me all the tips and tricks to using Scrivener, and for being my cheerleader, writer to writer.

To Francisco Reynoso, for providing graphics and always "getting" my design visions. You're the best. To my colleagues at Vantage Production who support me and allow me to flourish: Thank you.

To my family: Thank you and lots of love to Mom and Dad for showing me the value of hard work—and for providing me from an early age, with the foundation and drive that have led to the endless opportunities that I seek today. See? The English degree wasn't such a bad choice after all. To Michael and Kim for your love, support, and understanding, always.

Thank you to my dear friends and loved ones around the world who truly look out for me, love, understand, and propel me in everything I do, as crazy as it all may seem at times: you know who you are—all my love.

Thanks to the folks at NeueHouse and DT-UT for keeping me caffeinated, and being my alternate spaces to write this baby up. Though I did write this in various other parts of the world—when I wasn't busy working on Girl, Goin' Gone.

Finally, thank you to my all of my past mortgage clients in the metro Atlanta area. I am grateful for the opportunity to have learned from and worked in such a fast-paced, multifaceted, and demanding industry, and to have met so many professionals and families from all walks of life. Bad, good, excellent credit—*you* represent the readers of this book.

Without you, I wouldn't have been able to complete this project with such firsthand knowledge. I remember your faces, your stress, your joys, and I hope you are all doing well, and are staying blessed.

ONE

Scratching the Surface

Credit scores and credit reports. What's the big fuss about? Unfortunately, because of noisy TV commercials and radio advertisements, the very topic may have you running away from, rather than facing an important aspect of your financial portfolio.

Eyerolls and all, I believe that your credit score is your *greatest financial asset*, and by the end of this book you'll know why.

Where do you get a credit report? How do you get a credit score? Is it part of a credit report? If not, why not? What does a credit report include, anyway?

Why are companies allowed to pull your credit, and for what reasons are they using this information? Why should you bother, and what is the big deal?

Or is it that you are afraid to take those first steps in facing your credit issues and the topic just scares you?

Have no fear. *The Credit Cleanup Book* is here.

There's no reason for you to fear your credit report. Understanding exactly what your credit report shows and knowing your scores is not only empowering, but can be used as weapons in your financial arsenal when it comes to saving money and getting the best deals and rates on services, over the course of your life.

Just 100 points in a credit score can mean the difference between hundreds and thousands of dollars and time wasted to higher interest rates and fees.

Here's a simple example. Two homeowners are buying a home and need a $200,000 home loan. Borrower A, with a credit score of 760, qualifies for a rate of around 4 percent, where the monthly payment, before taxes and insurance, is approximately $955.

Borrower B, with a credit score of 660, qualifies for a rate around 5 percent, where the monthly payment is approximately $1075.

A credit score difference of 100 points costs Borrower B $120 *more* per month in interest fees. Also, after 5 years, Borrower B will pay $7,200 *more* than Borrower A.

Obviously, the figures grow the higher the loan amounts. If you continue qualifying for mortgages with lower credit scores, you'll suffer for each home loan received, every time.

Where the problem is truly apparent is reflected in credit card debt and fees. A person with excellent credit might have an average credit card APR of 15 percent charged on purchases. If he charges $5,000 and makes minimum payments toward the balance, he will end up paying more than double the original amount charged *and take almost 3 years to do it*!

But that's not all. The more shocking scenario is that someone with poor credit will likely have a 30 percent APR, and will have paid **25 times** the original $5,000 balance if he makes minimum monthly payments spread over three decades, to pay it all off. That ends up being over $120,000. This comparison should help crystallize just how much creditors receive on interest fees when consumers pay only the minimum amounts due monthly, and why a credit score matters. More on this is explained in Chapter 8, "Credit and Your Life."

You must be a step ahead of what lenders and service providers see when they consider your applications for money or products.

Now that we are roughly six years after the economic credit crisis and recession, Americans are borrowing again. The economy is slowly improving, as is the job market. People are regaining the confidence to buy and spend, and they are spending on major purchases such as homes and automobiles.

The Federal Reserve, under Fed Chief Ben Bernanke and now Janet Yellen, began tapering its economic stimulus efforts known as "Quantitative Easing" because it saw the signs of the United States' economic health bouncing back, albeit slowly, but it is has been happening since late 2013.

And according to a Federal Reserve report released in the first quarter of 2014, Americans in the last quarter of 2013 were once again seeking loans for new homes and automobiles,[1] almost with the same demand since the recession six years ago.

What does all this mean? It means that you should really be trying to understand where *you* stand. Because your credit score impacts you, your financial health, and most definitely your family's future.

Bravo to taking the first step in educating yourself by starting this book.

The purpose of this book is to make you aware of where you stand and help you get to where you want to be credit wise—to present yourself in the best light possible when it comes to your history and scores. If you want to improve your credit score, or remove negative information from your credit reports, I'll help you get there. I'm going to help demystify the process, and once you know what to anticipate, you'll find understanding and repairing credit to be less daunting of a project.

We'll get started with this chapter, by introducing the three credit reporting agencies (CRAs) that monitor your financial records, and learning a little history to boot. In Chapter 2, "Getting Prepared," I even provide some practical tips on getting organized and prepared for this process, as well as strengthening your mental focus to stay dedicated.

In Chapter 3, "The Credit Report," I'll provide information about ordering your reports and scores from not only the three major CRAs but also other sources that provide comparable information. They all have their differences, and we'll find out why.

For those who are hemming and hawing about getting your credit report for whatever reason, I'll tell you the simplest routes to get one. If you're nervous of what you might see, I encourage you to face down this fear—*now*. Just remember that whatever's there is there, and only *you* can change it for the better. It's your job to care, otherwise no one else will. Credit cleanup and positive credit maintenance are the baby steps toward financial empowerment, and you'll be glad you took them. With your credit scores and reports, ignorance is *not* bliss.

In Chapter 4, "The Credit Score," I'll break down the components and factors behind credit scoring. You may be surprised at what actions and credit items impact your score more than others, for example, recent versus older negative information, or how your overall debt usage is weighed.

In Chapter 5, "Checking and Correcting Your Credit Report," I'll help you analyze your credit scores, line items and history, and from here you'll be able to determine if your credit score is satisfactory, or what areas are in need of attention, correction, and improvement. Perhaps your score could be better once certain inaccuracies or outdated information are tackled. I'll take you through the dispute process with the CRAs to remove negative or adverse information.

In Chapter 6, "Improving Your Credit Score," my tips are actionable, easy to implement, and tested. By this point you'll understand what behaviors matter the most to credit scoring, and we'll try to apply these tips to our daily lives. I've used them myself, and am happy to share.

If your credit scores are suffering in large part due to the amount of debt you have accrued, Chapter 7, "Managing Debt," explains the various debt management strategies, including Do It Yourself (DIY) debt settlement or bankruptcy. You'll also learn about your rights and whether they're being violated by creditors and collectors according to the Fair Debt Collection Practices Act.

I firmly believe that you should know what happens when companies, utilities service providers, and lenders are evaluating when they pull your credit report, and I address credit qualifying criteria in Chapter 8, "Credit and Your Life."

If you're gearing up to buy a home, as many in postrecession 2014 are doing once again, we'll look at how banks and lenders have changed their qualifying guidelines for prospective mortgage applicants. If 2013 is repeated—should demand outweigh the supply of available, existing homes—you're going to need a solid preapproval before you go home-shopping. You can't get a stellar preapproval without decent credit.

Chapter 8 also discusses how your credit is evaluated while seeking employment, applying for insurance, getting a new apartment lease, or setting up utilities and services. Your credit score matters, and a healthy one will secure you the best deals, interest rates, and apparently even now, a potential life partner.

Finally, credit awareness and repair aren't sufficient to a promising credit future. After all the hard work and effort put into obtaining, learning about, and working on your credit, in Chapter 9, "Practice Makes Habit," I'll leave you with the latest and greatest tools to send you off in style. You'll learn about new budgeting and money management tools, and about the positive credit and money behaviors to avoid detrimental consequences.

If you find out your credit is not so great, then my goal is to help you repair and improve it. If your credit is already decent, I want to tell you how to make it excellent. If you've got excellent credit and aren't sure how certain financial decisions or actions will impact your credit score, I hope I can dispel myths or provide some clarity toward positive credit behaviors in the short and long term.

I truly believe a credit score is an undeniable Darwinian force—similar to how top SAT scores open doors for students to the best universities—top credit scores get you a company's best services and rates. Top credit scores put you in favor when seeking out leases and services. Consider having a top credit score as being in the exclusive club in the game of life, where success depends on how well one survives the pits and puzzles of the credit game.

Having a low credit score, though, is no game. It's a harsh reality that can cost dearly in missed opportunities, higher fees, and a lot of wasted money over a lifetime—but only for as long as you allow it to.

It's time to establish your greatest financial asset: your credit score.

While the idea of having your whole financial character being reduced down to a three-digit score is downright dehumanizing, that is exactly what happens when you ask a bank to lend you its money or a utility company to use its services. Everyone from banks, investment houses, mortgage and auto lenders, even cable and cellphone companies, want assurance of your ability to pay what is owed in a *timely* manner.

The Credit Cleanup Book will help you:

- Obtain your credit reports with scores
- Find out where you stand
- Contact credit bureaus or creditors to correct and remove negative information
- Understand your rights with regard to your credit report and debt collectors
- Understand positive credit behaviors and credit metrics
- Use the best tools for credit success

Just as I've used my own tips to improve my credit, I also coached many clients on these same tips as a former mortgage loan originator. I now want to provide you with invaluable and practical solutions to help achieve and keep higher credit scores.

So let's get started toward building our greatest financial asset.

A BRIEF AND NOT TOO BORING HISTORY OF CREDIT

Let's scratch the surface. First, it helps to know the names of the three main credit reporting agencies that are collecting and reporting information about you, also known as CRAs and credit bureaus. They are Experian, Equifax, and TransUnion, and they are regulated by the Fair Credit Reporting Act (FCRA). They also comprise a global, billion-dollar industry of credit scoring, reporting, and data warehousing.

Each CRA has a massive database, which consists of information on payment histories and financial records on hundreds of millions of consumers, on a frequent, usually monthly basis.

Every month, financial institutions or creditors send the CRAs credit files which include consumers' account numbers, types of credit (e.g., mortgages, credit card loans, and automobile loans), outstanding balances, collection actions taken against them, and bill payment histories.[2]

This data, I suspect much like the various Facebook data that advertisers find so valuable—for instance how often people are logging in, how long they're online, which companies they "like," and what other sites they access using the "Facebook Sign In" functionality—simply gives companies' marketing departments fodder to learn about your consumer behaviors.

The difference is that this data is used to determine someone's creditworthiness when he or she applies to borrow any money or use most services. It's your track record of how well or badly you've paid things on time, to whom, and for how much. This data is also sold to financial institutions, which, upon seeing your consumer history and the types of credit or debts you've had, will solicit you with deals and offers they think might suit your needs—deals you "can't refuse."

The Credit Bureaus

The history of credit reporting and scoring isn't so boring—honest. It's actually quite compelling and fascinating, considering it tracks the rise of the companies that are now gathering, reporting, and selling information about you, so that other companies can judge you by it. Really.

Back in the day, legend has it that when people purchased on credit, banks would keep internal ledgers on their clients' individual payment histories, and then exchange these client reputations with other banks. Imagine the administrative paperwork involved there, *way* before the Excel spreadsheet was even a twinkle in Bill Gates' eyes.

Equifax

The first CRA was Equifax, or what was then known as Retail Credit Company. Born in Atlanta, Georgia in 1899—where it is still headquartered today—Equifax started as a business-to-business data provider for life, auto, medical, and insurance policy applicants.

Nowadays, Equifax sells information, software, analytics, and consumer and business credit reports primarily to insurance and health care providers, utilities companies, government agencies, and financial institutions.

Equifax's consumer credit unit (the division which concerns average consumers like us) only started in 1999, and it offers what we mainly purchase in the form of products like credit reports, and services like credit fraud and identity protection monitoring.

TransUnion

Created in 1968 as a holding company, which then acquired a credit bureau, TransUnion has evolved over the years in its business-to-business products. TransUnion was actually at the forefront of technology, enabling tape-to-disc transfer of consumer data, as well as creating the first online information storage and retrieval data processing system, which drastically sped up lending decisions. Its consumer business, started in 2002, offers credit products like credit reports.

Experian

Technically the youngest of three bureaus by name only, Experian is a result of over a hundred years of mergers of both U.K. and U.S. data and retail companies, most notably TRW Credit Group, which rebranded as Experian in 1996. Since then, Experian has shed its parent company, the United Kingdom's Great Universal Stores (GUS), listed itself as a public company on the London Stock Exchange, and continues on its path to global information domination, by recently acquiring Brazil's largest credit bureau, Serasa, in 2007.[3]

Credit Scoring Is Born

In 1956, an engineer named Bill Fair and a mathematician named Earl Isaac founded the firm Fair Isaac and Company. Together, the pair worked hard to convince lenders that their mathematical formulas were the key to generating more reliable data from consumer credit histories.

By the 1960s, controversy was surfacing over what was contained in the CRAs' reports. People suspected that their credit reports were being used against them. They felt that lenders and businesses were denying them crucial services and opportunities, and leaving them largely in the dark with no rights to see what was in their personal files.

Perhaps this was largely due to the fact that CRAs back then were concerned mainly with negative financial information, as well as lifestyle information culled from newspapers and other sources—even information as personal as sexual orientation, drinking habits, and cleanliness.[4]

So Fair and Isaac came along with their algorithms, which looked past age, race, or gender discrimination. Their models could do substantially better at predicting an applicant's creditworthiness and tendencies to default faster than any human being could. A formulaic decision also couldn't play on human emotion and judge anyone based on bad teeth, breath, hair, clothes, or whatever other irrelevant credit criteria the loan decision makers were using as qualifying metrics at the time.

With their formulas, aided by superfast computer processing, what is today's billion-dollar credit industry was born.

In 1989, Fair Isaac and Company formally introduced its FICO score, which served as the formal basis for the loan decisions of banks and lenders. With computerized scoring, lenders could finally use empirical methods to determine consumers' credit worthiness.

As Liz Pulliam Weston, MSN Money's Personal Financial Columnist, stated, "Credit scoring, aided by ever more powerful computers, was also fast. Lending decisions could be made in a matter of minutes, rather than days or weeks."[5]

The Love Affair: FICO + CRAs

All three credit bureaus incorporated FICO's formulas into their credit scoring models. There's a misnomer that a "FICO score" represents or is tied to a *single* credit bureau, and this is simply inaccurate. All three credit bureaus use FICO's original data modeling within their credit scoring methods, but each in their own way, assigning greater weight to certain components over another. Which is why, if you've pulled your credit report previously, you get three *similar, but not identical*, scores. How credit is scored is further discussed in Chapter 4, "The Credit Score."

To add confusion to the process, each bureau's FICO scores have taken on nicknames of their own. Because of effective marketing by the CRAs and lending industries, we now have so many credit score names and types thrown at us that it's easy to lose track of what's what.

A Fashion Analogy

One way to think of it would be like this: The CRAs are three separate denim companies that make jeans. They sell plain jeans, but they also sell jeans with a special FICO thread. The special FICO thread is what makes the three denim companies' *premium* jeans authentic to retailers.

Of course, each denim company (CRA) has designed different shapes and styles in how and where they place this special FICO thread on their jeans, but they all end up looking very close to each other, just with minor differences.

The three CRAs' jeans with FICO thread have become so popular they're becoming even better known by the names of their premium jean lines: Beacon, PLUS, and Empirica jeans.

Although consumers can still get jeans from other companies without this FICO thread, maybe even at way less cost, and maybe without the fit or hug that the FICO-threaded jeans will provide, they'll be satisfied with what they get because the jeans look so close and are good enough for everyday and going-out wear. Heck, there's even a way to merge the best of all three denim companies' jean fabric, with the special FICO thread, into one. That would be the special (and pricey) tri-merge jean with that FICO thread.

FICO Score Aliases and Ranges

Hopefully the above helps you think about it all in a different way. But it's true. Over the years, the CRAs' individual FICO scoring models have earned nicknames in their own right. Whereas a FICO score is just really based on the original mathematical algorithms that serve as the basis from which most credit is modeled, the CRAs named their proprietary FICO score models with the following titles, as well as their unique credit scoring ranges:

CRA	FICO Score Name	Score Range
Equifax	Beacon	300–850
Experian	PLUS	330–830
Transunion	Empirica	400–925

If you've recently applied for a loan and the loan representative said, "Your 'Beacon' score is 745," then it means that the lender consulted Equifax for a credit report and score. The Beacon score is simply Equifax's FICO score for its consumer unit.

To spur up competition against FICO, the three CRAs actually collaborated to create the VantageScore model in 2006. They touted this score to be a more innovative and consistent approach to scoring. The VantageScore's scoring methodology primarily mirrors FICO's model, and also offers a letter grade on top of a numerical grade. But, it still hasn't quite pushed the FICO score off its throne. The FICO score is simply the most long-standing and entrenched model that has been in use by lenders. Also, when loans (like mortgages) are packaged together and sold as investments to buyers on Wall Street, their faith in the quality of those investments largely relies on the FICO scores used to underwrite and qualify those mortgages.

As a result, we won't focus too much on VantageScore in this book. After all, according to a Consumer Financial Protection Bureau report from September 2012, scores developed by Fair Isaac Corporation (FICO) accounted for over 90 percent of the market of scores sold to firms in 2010 for use in credit-related decisions.

Three Sides to the Story

One report does not a whole financial picture make. Regardless, many times service providers and even some lenders will order only a single report from a CRA to base their decisions. That's equivalent to a person judging a news story, tabloid, lovers quarrel, or any other situation based on only one side of the story. He may not receive the most thorough, accurate, well-rounded, or fair representation of a situation, but it may suffice depending on how much he wants to know. Single versus tri-merge reports are explained further in Chapter 3, "The Credit Report."

Simply put, many companies, particularly utilities companies or service providers, may only consult with one credit bureau to determine your creditworthiness. When I bought my first car in 2003 and a second in 2005, only a single credit report was pulled on my behalf when I was applying for auto loan financing.

When applying for a mortgage, which is asking for a lot more money than a car, the trifecta of credit data from the CRAs is always culled together so that the lender can have the full picture of the prospective borrower's credit history. Where one report may not suffice, the lender will want the full background on the loan candidate, which is wise considering that data may vary depending on factors as simple as the candidate's geographical location, bureau to bureau.

But Wait, There's One More

There is a lesser known credit agency out there, and it goes by the name of Innovis. Started in 1970, in addition to "credit reporting for more than 200 million consumers," Innovis also provides identity verification, fraud prevention, receivables management, and credit information, according to its website.[6] While the credit reporting part may resemble the functions of the big three, Innovis operates quite differently with the way it handles data—one reason it is not always recognized as a standard CRA.

According to the credit expert John Ulzheimer's SmartCredit blog, "Innovis receives credit information from credit grantors but not from all sources reporting to the big three credit reporting agencies. It does not sell credit reports for credit granting purposes and does not offer a credit score. They also sell pre-approved lists of consumers for offers of credit and insurance."

Ulzheimer, who is also the President of Consumer Education at SmartCredit.com, maintains that Innovis was originally going to be the negative bureau, reporting only negative credit information such as past due accounts. However after pulling his own Innovis report, he wrote on his blog that most of the data on it was mortgage-related, and since neither he nor a colleague who pulled her Innovis report had any previous negative credit such as collections or public records, he could not verify if this information was present or not on Innovis reports.

So the fact that Innovis doesn't sell your information for solicitors, doesn't score, and provides identity verification and receivables management makes it quite a different CRA. Innovis is, however, still regulated by the FCRA, and should your curiosity pique over what your Innovis report holds, you are entitled to one free credit report which can be requested directly from its website at www.innovis.com. The first one's free, and additional copies vary in costs by state.

CONSUMER PROTECTIONS

With the rise of credit reporting agencies collecting various data, and the scoring and decisions on loans taking place behind the scenes, consumers began to demand answers to what seemed very vague and hidden business inner workings.

They wanted to understand the discrepancies between credit card and home loan applications, as well as the criteria for which they were being approved or declined.

According to the Electronic Privacy Information Center,

By the 1960s, significant controversy surrounded the CRAs because their reports were sometimes used to deny services and opportunities, and individuals had no right to see what was in their file.

There was abuse in the industry, including requirements that investigators fill quotas of negative information on data subjects. To do this, some investigators fabricated negative information, and others included incomplete information. The CRAs were maintaining outdated information, and in some cases, providing the file to law enforcement and to unauthorized persons. Public exposure of the industry resulted in congressional inquiry and federal regulation of CRAs.[7]

The Fair Credit Reporting Act (FCRA)

The controversy led to a congressional inquiry, and in 1971, Congress passed the Fair Credit Reporting Act (FCRA), which for the first time established a framework for fair information practices to protect privacy and promote accuracy in credit reporting.

Consumers finally gained the right to view, dispute, and correct their records, and CRAs began to add positive financial history to the normally bleak reports, which up until then reported only negative information. Consumers also benefitted from the first official guidelines for fair practices in regard to the use of credit scoring. Finally, a process around scoring, reporting, obtaining, and disputing credit became clearer.

According to the EPIC,

Shortly after the FCRA took effect, the CRAs were pursued for violations of numerous provisions of the Act. As recently as January 2000, the three CRAs paid $2.5 million in a case settlement brought by the FTC.

Comprehensive amendments to the FCRA were made in the Consumer Credit Reporting Reform Act of 1996 (P.L. 104–208). The Amendments contained a number of improvements to the FCRA, but it also included provisions that allow affiliate sharing of credit reports, 'prescreening' of credit reports (unsolicited offers of credit made to certain consumers), and limited preemption of stronger state laws on credit.[8]

Even in recent years the Federal Trade Commission continues to legislate by the FCRA, suing the three major CRAs for almost $3 million in civil penalties. But it doesn't stop with just the CRAs—the FCRA's rules also apply to any information providers. The FTC sued a major consumer data broker, ChoicePoint Inc. and made them pay $15 million in penalties and consumer refunds for not screening prospective subscribers before selling them sensitive consumer information. The FTC has also charged companies with furnishing inaccurate information to CRAs.[9]

The Fair and Accurate Credit Transactions Act (FACTA)

In 2003, amendments were made to the FCRA, largely to address the alarming rise and continued reports of identity theft. As a result, the Fair and Accurate Credit Transactions Act (FACTA) was created. The act added a number of improvements to credit reporting law, including the right for consumers to receive free annual credit reports. On these credit reports, consumers were also given rights to place fraud alerts in case they became victims of identity theft.

To this day, many consumers are unaware of the "one-free-credit-report-per-year" benefit, perhaps because the onus is on them to request their personal reports. This could also be due to the amount of noisy mixed messages they receive, in the form of radio and television advertisements, alerting them to the plethora of credit reporting and monitoring products available.

Another tenant of FACTA was the requirement of merchants and retailers to truncate credit card account numbers from cardholder receipts at point of sale. Back in the day, if you dropped one of your credit or debit card receipts, a thief could have picked up that receipt and stolen your full credit card number and expiration date. FACTA changed that and enforces this rule with a fine of $100 to $1,000 per violation—and has been very successful, particularly when people band together in class-action lawsuits to face off against violators.

Rise of Consumer Debt and Credit Crisis

Once lenders grasped the idea of credit scoring, they didn't let go. Many would argue that credit scoring was too savvy, and enabled the rise of American consumer debt in the 1990s, given the banks' abilities to make snap judgments on issuing credit to qualified loan applicants. With credit scoring, an applicants' stellar credit history was sufficient proof of the likelihood that borrowers would make good on their loan commitments in a timely manner.

And since banks make money by lending money, the more risk-free debt they could dole out—in anticipation of the repayments of this debt plus interest over a period of time—the more money they could make for themselves.

Credit scoring has also been accused as the culprit in the most recent financial crisis, which had its beginnings in 2006. Critics have pointed to the failure of credit-scoring formulas, since the soaring number of borrowers who defaulted on their mortgages provided some evidence that perhaps scoring didn't work as well as it should.

To this criticism Fair Isaac and Co. responded that credit scores were designed only as part of a larger decision-making system, where lenders should also take just as many factors into account, such as the borrower's income, assets, other debts, and ability to repay the loan. And although credit scoring was probably the most significant factor in a candidate's loan application, if other large pieces of the puzzle didn't match up, then the full picture would be left incomplete.

Having been a loan originator myself, this much is true, except in the cases where the lenders' products didn't require income and asset documentation as a direct result of the strength of a borrower's credit scores.

As far back as 2005, the acting U.S. Comptroller of the Currency Julie Williams was warning lenders that they were relying too much on risk-factor shortcuts such as credit scores that focus on past credit performance, without considering the borrowers' ability to repay the new debt they were taking on.

Looking back, there were many contributors to "the perfect storm." Lenders became more and more creative about what they deemed acceptable underwriting guidelines and began lowering standards way outside of the conventional standards most lenders had traditionally banked on.

Lenders stopped requiring verification of certain aspects of a borrower's portfolio and stopped considering what could happen if the mortgages' rates adjusted higher amidst a changing housing climate. The credit crisis happened due to an arrogant assumption on many parts that housing appreciation and robust housing markets would continue along their heady path.

Lenders issued 100 percent home loan financing for borrowers who either had no money down, had mediocre credit, or both. This financing came with interest rates that were only locked for the first two, three, or five years. After the lock term the rates could rise as could the mortgage payments, resulting in a refinance as the only option to get out of the mortgage. But soon enough, even refinancing wasn't an option for many.

Investopedia defines credit crisis as "a crisis that occurs when several financial institutions issue or are sold high-risk loans that start to default. As borrowers default on their loans, the financial institutions that issued the loans stop receiving payments. This is followed by a period in which financial institutions redefine the riskiness of borrowers, making it difficult for debtors to find creditors."[10] To explain it further, it states,

> In the case of a credit crisis, banks either do not charge enough interest on loans or pay too much for the securitized loan, or the rating system does not rate the risk of the loans correctly. A crisis occurs when several factors combine in the marketplace, affecting a large number of investors.
>
> For example, banks will charge teaser rates on loans, but when the initial low payments change, they become too high for borrowers to pay. The borrowers default on the loans, and the loan's collateral

value simultaneously drops. If enough lending institutions reduce the number of new loans issued, the economy will slow down, making it even harder for other borrowers to pay their loans.

The credit crisis crippled our nation, bringing housing and new construction to a screeching halt in many major U.S. cities. As industries and the businesses relying on them slowed down, employees were laid off, and the after effects of this national correction are still being felt today. It would be roughly five years later in 2013 before any signs of economic health. In early 2014, lenders who were scared into tightening their lending guidelines had only just begun lending again, and borrowers, practically five years after the crisis, began getting comfortable with borrowing again.

The New Guard: Dodd-Frank

In an answer to the credit crisis, Congress passed the Dodd-Frank Wall Street Reform and Consumer Protection Act of 2010. This bill aimed to require more transparency on the part of various financial products being traded, as well as safeguards to prevent further major bank bailouts.

But furthermore, the bill created the Consumer Financial Protection Bureau (CFPB), which now also monitors the credit reporting industries. To specifically address the mortgage industry since its practices contributed so greatly to the most recent recession, in early 2014 Dodd-Frank also enacted a controversial new standard for lenders when underwriting and approving new mortgage loans. This additional scrutiny addresses a borrower's ability to repay a mortgage and is addressed in detail in the section, "This Is Now: New Mortgage Rules, New (Safer) Subprime," in Chapter 8.

According to the CFPB's website: "Congress established the CFPB to protect consumers by carrying out federal consumer financial laws. Among other things, we:

- Write rules, supervise companies, and enforce federal consumer financial protection laws
- Restrict unfair, deceptive, or abusive acts or practices
- Take consumer complaints
- Promote financial education
- Research consumer behavior
- Monitor financial markets for new risks to consumers
- Enforce laws that outlaw discrimination and other unfair treatment in consumer finance."[11]

How well the CFPB operates remains to be seen, since it is a fairly nascent yet already fully staffed organization. The CFPB takes direct submissions from consumers as well as whistleblowers. You can submit a complaint if you've had an issue with a financial product or service, which they claim they will forward to the company to get a response from them. (For complaints go to http://www.consumerfinance.gov/complaint/.)

In addition to consumer complaints, the CFPB also fields whistleblower tips. If employees at companies suspect unethical business practices they can submit anonymously to whistleblower@cfpb.gov or call (855)-695-7974.[12]

THE CREDIT REPORTING TRAIL

When companies and lenders pull your credit report, they are determining whether they:

1. want you as their customer,
2. want to grant you their services or lend you money, and
3. believe you can pay them back on time for the money borrowed and services used.

A credit report provides a glimpse of your debts owed, as well as a look at your money management behaviors over time. Lenders and companies won't give you what you want (and in most cases, what you can't live without) unless you've demonstrated an ability to responsibly manage and handle certain financial liabilities.

It's your right as a consumer to understand what companies are discovering about you when you're applying to borrow money or obtain services. This ranges from how well you've paid your bills and the types of liabilities or debts you've had, including your mortgage, credit cards, student loans, auto loans, and merchant cards (also known as major retailer credit cards like those for furniture, electronics, and clothing stores), as well as any information on file in public records, such as liens and judgments filed against you, and any bankruptcies or foreclosures in your name.

Many times—and I mean *many*—there is significant erroneous or outdated information on credit reports, which is why it's crucial to be aware of what's showing on your reports, and preferably on an annual basis. Checking your personal credit may also become a frequent necessity if you are preparing for a major purchase, such as buying a house or car. Or a boat perhaps? Which rings in the expression, "The best day in a man's life is the day he buys a boat. The second best day is the day he sells it." But really. Again, *YOU are the owner of your credit data, and if you don't care about your credit report and score, no one else will.*

How Your Actions Are Tracked, Compiled as Data, and Sold

The credit reporting trail starts with you. The minute you inquire about or open new credit, how you repay that credit eventually winds up on a credit report. But how does it all get there? This in itself is somewhat tricky. Because within the credit reporting system is a huge web of creditors, subscribers, members, associations, and agencies that are linked because of the incredible value of your consumer financial data.

You create the data, and everyone else captures it, reports it, passes it on, and sells it to one another. These processes and the layers involved are what make credit reporting the billion-dollar industry it is today. Note that aside from you being the data instigator in this process, the long list of data followers never anticipated for you to be actively involved anywhere else along the process, particularly not in monitoring or questioning their analysis of your behaviors and actions.

Remember that the credit bureaus all started as business-to-business organizations and facilitators of consumer data; only in the most recent decade and after FACTA passed and FICO started releasing public score data did the CRAs start direct-to-consumer divisions, allowing everyone to access their personal CRA information on file.

So who or what is logging your actions, and how does it ultimately show up on a credit report? First, large- to mid-sized creditors and debtors (which would be the likes of major banks and credit card issuers) *pay* the CRAs for the service of keeping track of their large volumes of consumer data, which includes payment histories. They are considered subscribers, who can not only report your consumer information, but also run credit checks.

According to former debt collector Dana Neal in his book *Best Credit*, it's unclear what the large or midsize subscribers pay the CRAs to do this; however, smaller creditors can also open up accounts with the bureaus by paying a setup fee of around $300, and then a monthly subscription fee of $50, which enables them to report at will.[13] To be considered, the company would have to manage and report data for a minimum number of accounts, anywhere from 100 to 500, depending on the CRA.

Underneath these subscribers are the CRA members, who only have the ability to pull reports. Neal asserts that because the CRAs are private companies, they aren't required to post specific guidelines for how they accept business accounts, other than claim that each account's eligibility is considered at their sole discretion.

For the companies that can't become subscribers or members, they can then turn to the many third-party agencies or associations who *are* subscribers and provide middlemen services by rolling up data from clients and reporting it to the CRAs on the nonsubscriber or nonmember company's behalf.

But what happens if individuals or small businesses are neither subscribers nor members, and aren't interested in joining the third-party associations to report data? If these companies can't report delinquent accounts or run inquiries they'll often turn to private collection agencies and other third parties—which also have subscriber accounts and report to the CRAs very diligently.

Add to this roster companies called Service Bureaus (some, which Neal states are owned by the creditors themselves) which aggressively scan public records on a regular basis in search of consumer names, addresses, and Social Security Numbers which, Neal asserts, have an accuracy that is suspect at best, often citing data that is transcribed and recorded inaccurately, with mixed-up names and SSNs, account numbers and amounts.

Do you remember the game as a child where you sat in a large circle and a person first whispered a phrase in one person's ear, and it went around the circle until the last person uttered the phrase out loud, which was nothing like the original? Don't let this be how your actions show up as the data on a CRA report.

With so many opportunities for errors in the amount of times your credit data changes hands from the moment it's created, it is up to you to ensure that what is presented at the end of the chain is correct and *presents you in the best light possible.*

TWO

Getting Prepared

Before we dive into getting our credit reports and scores and applying the cleanup strategies provided throughout this book, you may be interested in some tips and tools to get organized, and more importantly, focused.

For those of you who may not wish to learn about focus, goal setting, and personal productivity, please feel free to skip this chapter and get right to ordering your credit report.

The credit cleanup process requires tenacity, persistence, and diligence. The more work you have to do, the more you've got to stay focused and committed. The credit rules are written with such legalese and complexity that no average person in his or her right mind would attempt to dissect it. Unless you're a credit attorney or, like me, you worked directly or indirectly with the industry, and learned to play the game to win.

This section can help if you have a mental block toward setting and keeping goals, or can't find the time to begin at all. I consulted some esteemed colleagues and brought in their expert tips and strategies on not only *setting* attainable goals, but also *finding the time to achieve them* and *seeing them through to completion*. In this chapter I also provide some practical organization tips, since the nature of the information in your credit report is personally sensitive and should be kept as secure as possible.

Parkinson's Law states, "Work expands to fill the time allowed." Well that's dedicated to procrastinators like me and many of you, and it translates to, "We don't get off our butts until we have to." But let me stress that with credit cleanup, time is really of the essence. As we saw in Chapter 1, the longer you wait to confront your credit history, the more money you're potentially losing to higher interest and annual percentage rates (APRs), as well as falling victim to higher fees on various services. You're also bearing the brunt of the many nonmetric or *qualitative* unknowns impacted by having a poor credit profile, such as your job candidate profile when seeking new employment, as discussed in Chapter 8, "Credit and Your Life."

The absolute worst thing for me to hear would be that you begin this process and then quit halfway. Doing so will do you absolutely no good, and I don't want it to happen because ultimately everyone deserves to understand, improve, and have the best credit he or she can have. It's up to you. And if this hasn't been drilled into your head already: if *you* don't care about your credit, then no one else will.

Perhaps you fear the unknown work that lies ahead, or the thought of undertaking such a task overwhelms you. The positive reinforcement you find in this chapter will help get you on track.

Before you even picked up this book, credit cleanup may have seemed a daunting process, but it doesn't have to be, and really isn't once you know the steps, procedures, terms, and what to expect. Please know that there are many, *many* others out there in your shoes, and that you've got myself and the people who have contributed to this book all rooting for you. With advice, understanding, preparation, and putting yourself and your goals first, I believe anyone can attain any goal set in life.

You've taken the first step by opening up this book. So, take time to look over the practical and mental strategies below to start your journey on the right footing.

THE PRACTICAL

Let's stop a minute. That credit history stuff probably got you all excited and ready to start down the road to getting (and repairing, if it needs repairing) your credit score. If you're the most organized, productive, and efficient person who can stay focused on any task until completion, then skip this chapter.

However, if you're like most people who have a long list of daily to-dos, can't find the hours in the day for personal tasks, or get overwhelmed and distracted easily, then read on for some great practical organization tips, as well as some helpful mental productivity and focus tips.

One reality that you must face is that if you're due for some credit repair work, then it will be *work*. It will require your attention, commitment, and focus; otherwise you will not get what you want from the process. If anytime you feel overwhelmed or unsure how to get back on track, come back to this chapter, and I'm sure you'll again find some helpful ways to stay on track.

Getting Organized

Credit cleanup requires a basic level of paper and file organization, either physically or digitally. If you're like me, then you may often switch between viewing shorter documents online or on a monitor and reading longer documents on paper in hard copy.

Credit reports are lengthy and range from five pages in length or more. On the other hand, creditor correspondence may just be a couple of pages. Whether you prefer hard copy or digital file storage, remember that credit reports and related documents contain *very* sensitive data, so security here is absolutely key. Here are some organization tips:

Hard-Copy/Paper Organization

If you're going to manage your paperwork offline, then I recommend any binder or folder to keep your worksheets, credit reports, and correspondence organized. I would also advise keeping your documents in a safe or locked filing cabinet, especially if you share a living space or office with others.

Never throw out any credit-related document without first shredding it. Dumpster divers are out there ready to steal your identity and are on the lookout for any sensitive information such as your social security number, date of birth, addresses, and any major credit card account numbers. Invest in a great crosscut shredder; you'll be glad you did.

Digital Organization

For a greener approach, digital options now enable managing and storing important files either on your computer or electronically in the cloud. These days, since many credit reports and disputes can be requested, processed, and viewed online, it is entirely possible to manage all credit paperwork digitally, as long as you keep security top of mind.

Personal Laptop or Computer Security

If you're housing documents on a personal laptop or computer, then keep them in a secured or even encrypted folder. I've provided up to six tutorials for the two major operating systems on how to keep your computer files safe, at least from low-level snoopers. As of this writing, the links are accurate, however you can Google this process or the associated keywords, should they go out-of-date. Remember that all links mentioned in this book are updated regularly on the website, tccbonline.com.

For Mac Users

Encrypting your files with the Disk Utility is fairly simple and can be used for financial documents. I would recommend testing this out a few rounds before moving documents here:

1. Lifehacker: http://lifehacker.com/5796988/keep-private-files-both-se cure-and-at-your-fingertips-by-putting-an-encrypted-disk-image-on-the-os-x-desktop
2. A YouTube video courtesy user "dell1032" showing this process: http://www.youtube.com/watch?v=7ymjeIlMYVE
3. The same process with a bit more complexity, courtesy technology blogger Aaron Parecki: http://aaronparecki.com/articles/2013/07/29/1/a-simple-encrypted-password-file-on-osx

For PC Users

Several methods exist here, depending on the age of your operating system:

1. For Windows 8, 7, and XP users: http://www.groovypost.com/howto/windows-8-7-efs-encrypt-files-folders/
2. Here's how to encrypt or decrypt a file, from the Windows site itself: http://windows.microsoft.com/en-us/windows/encrypt-decrypt-folder-file#1TC=windows-7
3. How to encrypt almost anything, according to PC World: http://www.pcworld.com/article/2025462/how-to-encrypt-almost-anything.html

Choosing Effective Passwords

As always, for your computer and any online site and especially those concerning private financial or payment information, choose unique passwords that do not resemble a sequence of numbers (1, 2, 3, 4 . . .) or easy words, your dog's name, your last name, or your street name, and try to always combine letters and numbers in big and small caps as well as unique symbols (#, $, %, *, etc.).

It is highly recommended that you put some of the above security tips into practice, especially if you keep very sensitive information such as tax returns, credit reports, and correspondence on your computer. The same applies if you share a desktop computer with anyone, say a roommate, and want to avoid people from snooping around.

If you keep everything on a laptop and frequent coffee shops or coworking spaces with public Wi-Fi hotspots or shared networks, then I strongly urge you to maintain your sensitive files in encrypted and secured folders. As a general note, be leery when using public Wi-Fi, as it is never the safest option, and any hacker sharing the network could potentially see what you're doing. If you can't avoid being on a public network, then avoid accessing sites containing personally sensitive information. This includes bank sites, where you enter log-in credentials, or any retailer shopping sites, where you would enter credit card information or PayPal information for purchases. I know that retailers claim they have the highest level of security, but you can never be too sure, especially in the aftermath of major retailers like Neiman Marcus, Target, and Toys "R" Us suffering massive data breaches during the late 2013 holiday shopping season.

What I *would* recommend if you're constantly on the move, or want your own dedicated Wi-Fi, is a mobile hotspot device. You can purchase a personal hotspot device with a 4G signal like Verizon's Mobile Jetpack, which transmits data somewhat speedily and more importantly, securely.

Cloud Security

If you're organizing your documents in the cloud, then I recommend a secure online storage site like Dropbox (dropbox.com), where you can organize your paperwork in multiple folders, and easily drag and update files to and from it. Dropbox claims its security to be pretty solid; however, always remember to set up a complex password.

I've also discovered that Evernote (evernote.com) is a great web tool for keeping up with bits and pieces of massive projects. Evernote's online software makes it easy to create folders with an unlimited number of notes inside each folder. Within the notes you can attach documents of every kind: photos, screenshots, links, PDFs, and more. The Evernote app is also user friendly and fantastically functional. For a small upgrade fee, Evernote adds an extra layer of security beyond simple sign-in credentials, which I'd highly recommend if you're planning on using Evernote for keeping any credit-related documents.

Now that the housekeeping part has been addressed, let's address mental housekeeping by getting your brain prepared and committed.

THE MENTAL

Successful money and credit management is a commitment to make to yourself, and accomplishing this is one of the most empowering feelings in the world.

Understand that it's going to require some diligence and willpower to convert new behaviors into lifestyle habits. Just like any change or new action you want to adapt into your life, you will have to ask yourself some important questions and believe in yourself to perform certain tasks.

I'd like to share some focus and productivity tips from a friend and colleague, Jason Womack. Jason's book, *Your Best Just Got Better*, was published in early 2012, and it remains for me one of the most practical, nonfluffy books on productivity and efficiency, which focuses on your best work and self.

Jason is a coach, mentor, and teacher, and through his coaching program (www.TimetoGetMomentum.com) he's helped top executives and employees at the world's leading companies improve their work/life balance, collaboration skills, and most of all, personal productivity and efficiency.

Jason walks his talk because he is so uncompromising in the way he's chosen how to live his life—by committing to doing what he loves—which conveniently is what he's great at.

In addition to overseeing Get Momentum, in 2007 Jason created #CoffeeChats, which are regularly scheduled meetings that have grown into an international phenomenon. At any of these worldwide #CoffeeChats, you're sure to find an awesome neighborhood coffee shop and anywhere from an intimate group of four to a larger assembly of Jason's followers—at one I attended in New York's West Village there were at least 20 attendees!

#CoffeeChats (www.coffeewithwomack.com) are always scheduled at the very beginning of the day before the workday, sometimes as early as 7 or 8 A.M. Each attendee comes prepared to discuss personal goals and work styles with his fellow group members. Jason leads the charge by asking pertinent questions about personal productivity and goal setting and always challenges the group with small exercises and takeaways to work on further. When you have a group of like-minded people who have all assembled for the purpose of personal improvement, you leave pretty inspired and ready to commit to your goals.

So, without further ado, below are some of Jason's tips, which you can put into practice to begin and ultimately achieve your credit reporting and financial goals.

Jason Womack's Focus and Goal-Setting Tips

From Jason's book *Your Best Just Got Better*, I've plucked some of the most pertinent tips on setting and achieving goals. Try to implement any of the following as you begin the journey for obtaining, improving, and maintaining your credit report and score.

A Focus-to-Finish Mind-Set

Let's get your mind focused. Credit cleanup is going to require a lot of focus, so we have to be ready when distractions and the temptation to multitask or overtask get in the way.

In his book, Jason provided the frustrating example of getting up to go do or get something, only to forget why you even got up and walked to another room in the first place! Trust me, plenty of times I've walked into another room or area, and when I got there I went completely blank.

Turns out, this may not be due to memory loss because you're getting old, or even short-term memory loss, but *entirely* due to simply having way too much on your brain and not being able to focus properly. For this, we must apply a focus-to-finish mind-set, by choosing one of the two options below the next time we come across a task or goal:

1. Stop and Do.
2. Stop, Think, Bunch, and then Do.

The first option, "Stop and Do," is exactly what it means. It means you get it done, right there and then, and it's finished forever. But, it's only feasible if the right time and place allow it. For example, if you want to order your credit report online, you're going to need a smartphone, tablet, or laptop. Regarding time, you're going to need approximately five to 15 minutes to enter all your data to obtain it.

With tasks that you can Stop and Do, there's no more lingering, thinking, should-ing, or anything. Taking that first step by stopping and getting your online credit report would be a great example of Stop and Do.

The second option, "Stop, Think, Bunch, and Do," comes into play when you think of a task that has many moving parts. These moving parts would be considered the "vertical" parts related to a task.

For example, if you're charged with arranging a dinner for a large group, the booking is the end goal. The multiple parts of the task, or the vertical tasks, include the following: gathering RSVPs, calling and speaking to the restaurant, arranging the menu and prices, reconfirming RSVPs, and so on. All these little tasks need to be "bunched" so that they can be attacked one by one. But when you've got them listed out accordingly and when the right time allows, you can attack them each with Stop and Do.

Credit cleanup will almost certainly be a mix of Stop and Do and Stop, Think, Bunch, and Do. Thinking about tasks in this way will help you develop that focus-to-finish mind-set.

Save It for Later

You're out and about, busy in your week or workday flow and then—*poof!*—a brilliant idea or something you want or need to do pops into your brain. You perhaps can't or wouldn't very well stop what you're doing to do it immediately, so Jason recommends that you scribble whatever it is down on a side piece of paper so that you can get to it later.

If you're running around, then record these thoughts and ideas in your smartphone's to-do list or notes area. Most phones, even the most basic models these days, have a very basic note-taking function. For smartphone users, I prefer the new Any.do app, which has an intuitive easy to-do list experience.

After years of scribbles on little pieces of paper that were gone with the wind in seconds, I finally found an app that's easy to record multiple layers of notes, with subfolders *and* syncs with my calendar. You can also voice dictate any items you want to add. It sure feels good when you strike out something your list and it stays crossed out, until you want to bring it back from the dead, or you can just delete it altogether. This feature is especially helpful for grocery lists full of items that you may want to re-purchase down the road; or for recurring work items and tasks.

By transferring these tasks and ideas from your mind to a notepad or your phone, you won't lose your focus on your task at hand, but rather have comfort that it's held for safekeeping later.

We, and especially me, sometimes suffer from shiny object syndrome, where our attention spans are so short and made worse with on-demand everything, facilitated by technology—and I've never been officially diagnosed with ADD. Above all news, texts, e-mails, streaming video, and calls, let's give these great ideas and things-to-do a chance for their deserved focus later on and not let them divert us from what deserves our attention *at that very moment.*

Let's not get sidetracked. Let's not totally interrupt our workflow on another existing task or project to work on something else right away. When you behave in a reactionary or putting-fires-out kind of way, it's not productive in the long run. It's always better to capture the thought and focus properly on it later. Your current project and this great idea both deserve your undivided attention at their proper time and place.

So next time you're sitting down at your desk with the intention of work, before you allow the temptation to Google something, catch up with friends on Facebook, or online shop for shoes, *don't.* Instead, put the phone on silent and leave it on the other side of the room. Take Jason's advice by scribbling down whatever it is you get the urge to look up, on a piece of scratch paper by your side. You'll see your time management improve if even in small increments, which brings me to the next section.

Everything in Increments

The easiest way that Jason knows how to get *started* doing things differently is to begin *slowly,* and practice with intention and deliberate focus. It's far better to take on just one new idea and spend precious energy and focus on it *every day* for a week, than to spontaneously decide to make several big changes, only to give up on them in 48 hours. Another profound takeaway from Jason's book is the fact that in any 24-hour day, you have only 96, 15-minute increments. A lot can be accomplished in just 15 extremely focused minutes.

Try it, and you'll be impressed with what you can accomplish by giving any task just 15 minutes of your *full* attention—which means *no* multitasking and *no* distractions.

This idea of short, focused blocks of attention is not a new concept. Experts often believe one works better by breaking up large-scale tasks requiring lots of concentration into short, manageable blocks of time. Back in the 1980s a man by the name of Francesco Cirillo coined the Pomodoro Technique of time management (www.pomodorotechnique.com), by breaking up work and study into timed, 25-minute bursts of focused activity and attention. A kitchen timer set for 25 minutes gets you going. At the end of the 25-minute block (or when you jump in your chair once the timer goes off), you take a five-minute break, then work toward completion of the first task, or finish that task and start on another. If you don't have a basic kitchen timer, you can also download a simple Pomodoro Timer desktop app called Focusbooster, available at www.focusboosterapp.com. The app will allow for a small timer in the corner or background of your computer as you work away.

As you begin the credit cleanup process, ask yourself which 15 (or 25) minute block(s) of your day can be focused on your greatest financial asset. As Jason says, "When you identify tasks that take too much time, and practice ways to work productively, effectively, and efficiently, you could easily net 1 to 3 extra 15-minute blocks of time each day. With 15 to 45 extra minutes tomorrow, and every day after that, imagine how much progress you could make towards your financial goals!"[1]

After all, once you pull your credit report and examine your credit history and scores, only you can determine how satisfied you are with what you see to date.

Experience Completion

As Jason stated in *Your Best Just Got Better:*

I know what happens when I experience completion: I feel a boost in confidence, interest, and energy. I love the feeling of having finished something, whether it's an article, a triathlon, or a seminar.

When we are managing time, we're managing much more than the tick-tock of the clock. We're managing our areas of focus and responsibility; we're fielding interruptions from others; we're listening to our own self-talk; and we're generating all kinds of other ideas. All the while, we're inhibited by very specific influencers to our productivity.

Imagine how incredible you'll feel once you've raised your credit score to where you want it to be. If you've ever felt the embarrassment or shame of being rejected for offers or credit in the past, then you won't have to again. Not only that, but you'll be able to get the best deals and rates available, which results in money-saving opportunities and benefits for as long as you keep your credit healthy. Now *that* feeling is a pretty fantastic feeling that you deserve—but it only comes with completion.

According to Jason, completing any goal comes with four key resources, which are time, energy, focus, and tools. They are interdependent, and only when you have the right balance and progression from one to the next, can you experience completion.

The Four Resources for Completion: Time, Energy, Focus, Tools

- Your ability to make the most out of your *time* is a function of the *energy* you have available to apply to your work.

- The *energy* you can apply to your work is determined by your ability to *focus* on your work. This helps you manage your priorities more effectively.

- Your ability to *focus* on your work is determined by the systems and tools you use to manage your responsibilities.

- When you use your *systems* and *tools* efficiently, you work in a more focused manner and habits of *completion* will begin to affect you and your team.

- With completion and accomplishment comes the result that you are using your time wisely.

Think about each of the resources clearly. You may have one without others and vice versa. If you've got all the time in the world but no focus, you're not going to achieve anything. If you've got all the tools at your disposal but you don't have the focus to use them, you're not going to achieve anything. If you are dog-tired from partying or working too much you're going to lack energy *and* focus.

Only when the four resources above act in harmony can you truly accomplish any goal, which in this case, is credit cleanup.

A Meditative Approach

In researching this book, one of the most driven people I know offered to provide some tips on mentally preparing for financial management. That was the professional meditation coach, Mary Joan Cunningham.

Now, before you think this has gotten all Kumbaya and unicorns, the steps below are not just reserved for meditating, but rather important steps to help with personal focus and goal-setting.

I do believe that meditation provides clarity, and that forms of it, with proper guidance, can allow you to embrace your full potential to overcome many mental obstacles in life. Even if you don't subscribe to it or plan on exploring its capability further, I think you'll agree with me that in any state of uninterrupted, quiet focus, where you have no outside noises disturbing you, is when you think most clearly. Ever heard the phrase "Sleep on it"? That's because sleep provides the rejuvenation and calmness sometimes necessary to approach issues head-on. A meditation session can provide equal results.

When Mary heard that I was writing this book, she immediately offered her assistance to help my readers set and attain their financial goals. One course of her guided meditation series already focused on financial freedom. So if you're feeling a little overwhelmed as to where to start and need some guided mental focus, take a look at her three simple steps to get started:

Mary Joan Cunningham's Tips for Clarity and Goal Setting

If you're reading this book, you already know you want to achieve better financial health. But what does that really look like or feel like? Here, Mary breaks down the ways you can make this desired goal your reality.

Success lies in bringing attention to specific desires and the focused actions that will yield positive results. By remaining "present" to each step of the path, we can create a truly dynamic shift in our personal finances. So let's get started:

Set a Specific Intention

Are you finally ready to do what it takes to up your credit score? Take a moment to set an intention for what you want to accomplish *first*. We often skip this initial step because when we get inspired, we feel invigorated to take on many challenges upfront and *all* at once. This uplifting energy can quickly give way to disappointment if we let overwhelm creep in.

So set yourself up for success by breaking down what you want into individual goals or intentions, and identifying in what order they should come. Be focused with each intention so that each is achievable. Immerse yourself in the proactive pursuit of each goal, letting yourself succeed with one, before moving on to the next.

To help "Set a Specific Intention," ask yourself the following questions:

What is your specific intention for credit cleanup?
Why do you want to clean up your credit?
Do you want to be debt free by the end of the year?
Are you planning to purchase a home?
Is it all of the above? Or something else?

If your desire is to clean up your credit, an example of a specific intention could be, "I want to be debt-free in a year."

You can take that intention one step further by clarifying and stating it as, "I will pay down the balance of each of my credit cards to 30 percent of their total available credit within five months."

Confronting and Releasing Fears

Now that you know what you want to accomplish, it's time to look at what's been prohibiting you from getting there. The likely culprit? Fear.

According to Mary, without realizing it, you may be toting around some really gnarly fears. Instead of ignoring them, it's vital to pay attention and listen to them. Trust her, they tell really interesting stories.

Some fears might go all the way back to childhood and have no relevance in our adult lives, *other than forming a very real barrier to success.* Perhaps you blame others or a previous event for your current situation.

Did you grow up thinking that you would never have enough because your parents favored the phrase, "Money doesn't grow on trees"? Or did you see the negative fallout of a relative who couldn't pay bills regularly and witnessed the havoc that this situation brought to his or her personal life, thus believing on some level you could end up the same way?

To some degree, are you blaming a previous life event for your current situation, thus letting your past define your future? Any number of fears and stories can be in your subconscious, diminishing your ability to move forward proactively and positively.

Realize that we humans favor habit, even in our thought patterns (hence, the term "patterns"), so if the path to financial health is uncharted territory for you, remind yourself that all of this might feel scary because your mind is (read: *you are*) choosing to go on autopilot and reverting to fear- or worry-based thinking out of sheer habit. Any time a fear or an "old story" comes in, use that as your opportunity to examine, expel, and move on. This will dynamically change your perspective on finances and your life overall.

Let go and move forward. After you hear the fear, allow yourself to release it—breathe it out.

To help confront and release your fears: At any time throughout your day—be it while you're working, lying in bed, swiping a debit or credit card and especially during the exercise outlined in the third step—take note of anytime you feel tightness, perhaps in your chest or your head, and anywhere you feel yourself clenching. Take a few deep breaths to move the tightness out and ask, "What is my fear in this situation?"

Breathe and listen to your body or the inner voice that answers this question.

After you acknowledge the fear, you must allow yourself to release it. On your next inhalation ask, "What is my truth in this situation?" and here's where you get to connect with your inner guide who knows that you're on the right path. Align with the best that you have within you to proceed on the path to success. Because if you're doing this exercise, the truth is that you're present to your financial reality and endeavoring to improve it. See this truth, and allow yourself to chart the way ahead.

Visualizing Success

Now that you've focused your intention and understand how to shred through old fears, give yourself time and space to do so daily. Even if for only five minutes, the time you invest to bring attention to this goal and dismantle any fears that might be creeping in around it will help you chart the way forward to financial peace of mind and success, in whatever terms you define it.

To visualize success:

- Start by grounding yourself and position with both feet planted firmly on the floor. Allow your eyes to close.
- Focusing your internal vision at the center of your forehead, envision your financial goal in the distance.

What does completion look like? What does it feel like? What will you be wearing when you accomplish this goal?

- While you visualize the achievement of this goal, connect with the positive energy around its successful completion.
- Keep this positive energy with you.

Give it a color, maybe red, the color of self-love and physical security. Or green, the color of abundant, selfless love. Or choose your own favorite color!

- Let this energy fill you, and again see the goal in the distance.
- Allow any fears to come up and announce themselves. Acknowledge them and release them.
- Come back to the abundant, positive energy and as you focus through your brows to the vision of accomplishment in the distance, feel your energy grow stronger and move through you.
- Begin to bring your awareness to where you are today and what next steps are illuminating to show you a path toward your goal.
- What is the next step? It can and should be really basic, totally attainable, yet maybe something you hadn't seen before.

Are you connecting with a positive energy of only buying what you can afford?

- What other next steps are lighting up for you? Does it feel aligned to get online and pay your utility bills now so you can determine how much cash is left to manage your month? Depending on your personal intention, these forward steps will vary, but will be similarly incremental and meaningful.
- Keep this energy with you. Begin to bring your awareness to where you are today and let the next steps become illuminated toward the positive feeling and financial goal.
- As you repeat this daily, each day you'll clarify your desire, bringing you that much closer to achieving it.

Your financial goals can and should be wildly positive and inspiring, but remember that this uplifting energy could easily give way to disappointment if we let overwhelm creep in. But you got this. Stay focused with each intention so that the goal is achievable, continue to root out old fears, and remain present to the illuminated small steps that are carrying you toward accomplishing your financial goals.

For more information, you can follow Mary's insights and her stories on Twitter by following @MeditatewMary.

Incredible meditative primer, right?

Jim Hartness and Neil Eskelin's Time Management Principles

I leave you with a passage from another favorite book of mine, *The 24 Hour Turnaround*. In it, Jim Hartness and Neil Eskelin use 24 chapters, for each hour of the day, to instill readers with positive lessons one can digest one hour at a time, daily. The book isn't meant as a sit-down read from front to back, but as a book where you read only a chapter at a time and ponder on it for that hour or as long as you need.[2]

Chapter (or hour) 13, titled, "How to Reorder Your Day," focuses on time management, with the following time management principles to help you prioritize as it relates to *your* personal time:

Live in the Present

It is vital to focus on the immediate time you've been granted. Not yesterday, which can't be changed, or in the future unknown, but *today.*

Place a Value on Your Activity

Know how much you're worth. Many who set their annual financial goals blindly fail to calculate what they need to achieve daily or hourly to reach it. When you determine the value of a minute of your life, you'll treat it with much greater respect.

Create a Written Daily Schedule

Plan and coordinate your actions. Do this beyond the 9-to-5 and take consideration for your personal well-being, by blocking time for reading or personal fitness and meditation.

Prioritize Your Tasks

Complete the hardest tasks first and with the most energy so the others gradually become easier to tackle throughout the day.

Make Effective Use of Short Periods of Time

Don't think about it, just do it. This directly echoes the importance of 15-minute blocks as Jason already mentioned. When you're riding the train, waiting in line or waiting for appointments and meetings to begin, always be working on a personal task list.

Don't Allow Others to Determine Your Schedule

You must be in charge of your day. Don't allow others to interrupt you with phone calls or e-mails—put your phone on silent or do-not-disturb mode, and place it facedown when you're in the middle of working. Request to be unlooped from unnecessary e-mail threads. Schedule meetings for less than the standard full hour. Be adamant about this.

Work Smart

Dale Carnegie once told the story of two woodchoppers. One worked hard all day long with no breaks whereas the other would take short breaks and a short nap after lunch. Both men yielded the same results. When the former asked how every time he looked around the other was sitting down, the latter simply replied, "Did you also notice that while I was sitting down I was sharpening my ax?"

Recognize Time Wasters

Acknowledge and avoid the behaviors that are wasting your time. Most times you already know your answer and how you wish to decide; don't let yourself fall victim to the habit of saying, "Let me think about it."

Focus on Personal Productivity

Hold yourself accountable for efficiency and machinelike results. You'll be amazed at what you can achieve when you light the fire up under your rump.

Do It Now

Now is the three letter word that can mean the difference between success and failure. This also mirrors Jason's advice to "Stop and Do," or "Stop, Think, Bunch, and Do." Likewise, Hartness and Eskelin say that when a piece of paper comes your way, always handle it in three steps:

1. Throw it away.
2. Take action on it.
3. File it.

IT'S TIME TO TURN YOUR CREDIT AROUND

The above steps, concepts, and tips are ways to help you get focused and committed. And while it may seem daunting—if at any time throughout this book and the process you get offtrack and need support to get refocused and energized, come back to this chapter of the book. As with any new behaviors, only practice and diligence will eventually make a habit. The trick is to start small and at *your* speed, even very slowly if you have to. Don't you think it's time you dedicated some minutes of your life to your greatest financial asset? I certainly do. Let's get started.

THREE

The Credit Report

Let's decipher this initially daunting, glorified spreadsheet. A credit report, at first glance, may look like a big grid of columns filled with text. Let's demystify it. Each section is relevant and serves its own unique purpose. And the intention of *The Credit Cleanup Book* is to make this process as painless and familiar as possible.

A credit report is a record of the entire history of your debts. It is also a snapshot of your balances owed on any lines of credit or debt you have, at this very moment.

Any time you provide your social security number (SSN) to borrow money or open a credit line—with the intent to purchase goods on that credit—this activity will be recorded on your credit report.

Likewise, as you pay toward a balance for an outstanding loan or credit card, this activity will be included on your credit report. If you have any derogatory credit, such as collections, liens, bankruptcies, and foreclosures, this is also included on a credit report. These primary components of the report are then followed by information regarding your most recent credit inquiries as well as name and address verifications.

SINGLE VS. TRI-MERGE CREDIT REPORTS

When prequalifying for loans and services, some lenders and service providers, like utilities providers, may only pull a credit report from a single CRA. This allows them to get a quick picture of a loan candidate, rather than commit to a full tri-merge report. By logic, single reports are also cheaper than tri-merge credit reports because they only contain data from a single CRA.

A single report, however, may not tell the loan candidate's full credit story, and any prequalifications or denials based on that report aren't considering other CRA data, which may be better or worse. A tri-merge report reconciles all three major CRAs' data into one file, for one total picture. Rather than consult three separate files, the data is merged in one report for reference.

Many times, a *negative* credit item reported by one bureau may actually show to be in *good* standing by the other two credit bureaus. And while the account might very well be in good standing, if a lender makes a decision based on a single CRA report that contains negative information, it is unlikely to offer the best outcome in terms of product, service or rate. The onus is always on the consumer to contact the credit bureau responsible, and demand for the negative item to be updated or removed from its records.

ACCURACY BY REGION

One practical reason for credit reporting inaccuracies by the CRA may simply be due to each bureau's geographical location in relation to the report holder. For instance Equifax is based in Atlanta, Georgia, whereas TransUnion is headquartered in Chicago, Illinois. A person living in the southeastern United States may simply have more information on the Equifax report than the TransUnion report.

Perhaps a judgment or lien filed in local courts shows on the person's Equifax report but is missing from the TransUnion report because of the processing time required for this data to reach TransUnion's records. Or perhaps a collection that was recently paid to a local property management company only flags on Equifax's report, but is still showing as unpaid on the TransUnion report, again, simply due to locality and timing. Perhaps Experian has updated a derogatory item to be current, while Equifax is reporting an outdated status. It is for these reasons that lenders use tri-merge reports for larger loan amount credit applications, such as for mortgages, so that they can have the total credit picture on that applicant.

INTRODUCING: BARRY BORROWER

Take a look at the sample credit report (Figures 3.1–3.3). It's a report for our friend Barry Borrower, in its entirety, with all the meaty parts of a credit report intact. Remember that all documents referenced throughout this book are also available as PDF worksheets which can be downloaded from www.tccbonline.com.

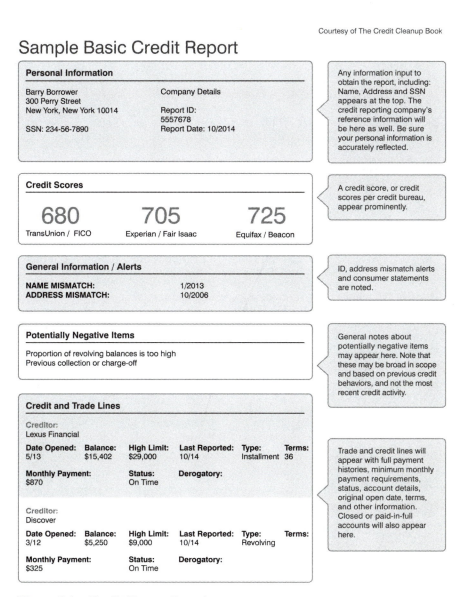

Sample Basic Credit Report

Personal Information

Barry Borrower
300 Perry Street
New York, New York 10014

SSN: 234-56-7890

Company Details

Report ID:
5557678
Report Date: 10/2014

Any information input to obtain the report, including: Name, Address and SSN appears at the top. The credit reporting company's reference information will be here as well. Be sure your personal information is accurately reflected.

Credit Scores

680
TransUnion / FICO

705
Experian / Fair Isaac

725
Equifax / Beacon

A credit score, or credit scores per credit bureau, appear prominently.

General Information / Alerts

| **NAME MISMATCH:** | 1/2013 |
| **ADDRESS MISMATCH:** | 10/2006 |

ID, address mismatch alerts and consumer statements are noted.

Potentially Negative Items

Proportion of revolving balances is too high
Previous collection or charge-off

General notes about potentially negative items may appear here. Note that these may be broad in scope and based on previous credit behaviors, and not the most recent credit activity.

Credit and Trade Lines

Creditor:
Lexus Financial

| Date Opened: | Balance: | High Limit: | Last Reported: | Type: | Terms: |
| 5/13 | $15,402 | $29,000 | 10/14 | Installment | 36 |

| Monthly Payment: | Status: | Derogatory: |
| $870 | On Time | |

Creditor:
Discover

| Date Opened: | Balance: | High Limit: | Last Reported: | Type: | Terms: |
| 3/12 | $5,250 | $9,000 | 10/14 | Revolving | |

| Monthly Payment: | Status: | Derogatory: |
| $325 | On Time | |

Trade and credit lines will appear with full payment histories, minimum monthly payment requirements, status, account details, original open date, terms, and other information. Closed or paid-in-full accounts will also appear here.

Figure 3.1   Credit Report Page 1

Credit and Trade Lines

Creditor:
Chase

Date Opened:	Balance:	High Limit:	Last Reported:	Type:	Terms:
4/10	$750	$4,500	9/14	Revolving	

Monthly Payment:		Status:	Derogatory:		
$25		On Time			

Creditor:
Bank of America Visa

Date Opened:	Balance:	High Limit:	Last Reported:	Type:	Terms:
2/08	$2,500	$8,325	10/14	Revolving	

Monthly Payment:		Status:	Derogatory:		
$175		On Time	30 Days, 6/10		

Creditor:
Sallie Mae

Date Opened:	Balance:	High Limit:	Last Reported:	Type:	Terms:
3/06	$39,934	$75,000	10/14	Installment	15

Monthly Payment:		Status:	Derogatory:		
$634		On Time			

Creditor:
MasterCard

Date Opened:	Balance:	High Limit:	Last Reported:	Type:	Terms:
1/06	$4,500	$6,000	10/14	Revolving	

Monthly Payment:		Status:	Derogatory:		
$175		On Time			

CLOSED

Creditor:
ABC Mortgage

Date Opened:	Balance:	High Limit:	Last Reported:	Type:	Terms:
5/06	$189,124	$215,000	12/13	Installment	360

Monthly Payment:		Status:	Derogatory:		
$1,255		PAID IN FULL			

Figure 3.2   Credit Report Page 2

Derogatory Information

COLLECTION:
Con Edison

Date Opened:	Balance:	Last Reported:
1/10	$262	2/10

Monthly Payment:	Status:
$25	PAID IN FULL

> Public Records, Collections, Charge-offs, Bankruptcies, Foreclosures and any other derogatory information are listed in this section, along with the respective status.

Inquiries

Capital One	3/2014
Best Rate Mortgage Company	1/2014
Best Buy	1/2013
Verizon Wireless	10/2012

> A list of the most recent requests for your credit history. Some reports may provide a more thorough list that separates inquires initiated by you, or by creditors who are screening to make credit offers.

Personal Statements

CONSUMER STATEMENT: PLEASE CONTACT ME AT 212-555-5555 FOR ANY NEW CREDIT ACCOUNT REQUESTS.

> Any personal statements provided to creditors to prevent consumer fraud, or any explanation on facts or conditions of any items on the credit report.

Personal History and Verification Data

Borrower, Barry
AKA
Borrowerz, Barry   SSN: 234-56-7890
NAME MISMATCH
1/2013

Borrower, Barry
AKA
Borrower, Baron   SSN: 234-56-7890
NAME MISMATCH
10/2012

Current Address:
300 Perry Street
New York, NY 10014
Reported 10/2012

Previous Address:	**Previous Address:**	**Previous Address:**
100 Fulton Street	250 Desbrosses Street	120 Peachtree Road
New York, NY 10038	New York, NY 10013	Atlanta, GA 30324
Reported 8/2009	Reported 10/2006	Reported 10/2006

> Any addresses, aliases and dates of birth reported by data providers, to further verify consumer information. Name, address or SSN mismatches may also be noted in this section.

Figure 3.3   Credit Report Page 3

No matter where *you* obtain your credit report, there will be certain constants within, which are personal information, credit scores (for reports with scores), credit and trade lines, potentially negative items, recent inquiries, and address and name history.

You'll notice that Barry's report is an example of a "tri-merged" report as mentioned earlier, which includes all three CRA reports merged in one file. When we order your credit reports in the next section, we can decide how we'll go about obtaining all three reports: separately or merged into one file. But let's now walk through the main sections of a sample credit report.

The Sample Credit Report

Personal Information

At the top of your credit report is the information that was provided to obtain it. Your full legal name, current address, and SSN (or a truncated version of your SSN) will appear in this section. Ensure that what appears in this section is as accurate as possible.

Depending on the company or CRA used to generate the report, a tracking number for your report may also show here, much like it does on Barry's report (Figure 3.4).

Figure 3.4   Sample Report: Personal Info

Credit Scores

For credit reports with scores, you'll see your three-digit credit score(s) for each credit bureau prominently located near the top (more details on credit scoring are discussed in the next Chapter, "The Credit Score"). For Barry's tri-merge report, looks like his three scores from the major CRAs are 680, 705, and 725 (Figure 3.5).

Figure 3.5   Sample Report: Credit Scores

General Information and Alerts

This section flags any name or address mismatches, fraud alerts, consumer statements, and other particulars tied to a personal credit report.

General Information / Alerts

NAME MISMATCH:	1/2013
ADDRESS MISMATCH:	10/2006

ID, address mismatch alerts and consumer statements are noted.

Figure 3.6   Sample Report: General info

We can see that Barry's report includes a name mismatch logged in January 2013 and an address mismatch in October 2006 (Figure 3.6). After we've reviewed the entire report, we can do some sleuthing to piece together why such alerts occurred, but first, let's understand why they occur at all.

NAME AND ADDRESS MISMATCHES

Don't be alarmed if you see the standard name and address mismatch alert on your personal report, as these mistakes occur quite frequently. What you *should* be concerned with, however, is whether a fraud alert or consumer statement appears, which we'll address shortly.

A *name mismatch* is quite common. For example, if a person's legal first name is *James* and a lender has pulled a credit report on James' behalf using his nickname *Jim*, then a name mismatch is triggered. It's as simple as that. Whenever data is entered that differs from the data on file in any way, or differs from your actual legal or birth name tied to your SSN, it is logged within the credit reporting data and history.

This also typically happens when a person goes by a middle name, for which a lender may input as the first name for credit report–pulling purposes, unaware of the name variation. A name mismatch alert is mainly to raise concern, should credit be pulled for someone whose name varies greatly from the actual name on the credit report. All first, middle, and maiden name variances are expanded upon and listed again later in the report, in the "Personal History and Verification Data" section, which we'll look at later to decipher Barry's alerts.

An *address mismatch* may be triggered when a person is attempting to set up, for the very first time, utility services at a new address because he or she has recently relocated. Since the new address is not yet recognized as the credit applicant's home address across any CRA data, an address mismatch may be flagged. Again, this alert, along with a name mismatch, is a common one; however, care should be taken in case of a new credit inquiry linked to a completely unfamiliar or foreign address.

While the sample report doesn't include any of these, a high risk fraud alert may show if any of the following has occurred:

1. A high number of recent credit inquiries, signifying fraudulent activity in the form of many attempts for new credit in a very short period of time.
2. The SSN isn't a standard issued number from the Department of Social Security.
3. The address used to obtain the reports appears linked to previous fraudulent activity or is not a standard residential address.

Of course, regarding the first scenario, while this practice is discouraged, someone could also be shopping around for preapprovals from mortgage lenders, which explains the frequent credit inquiries. During the mortgage process, lenders will also scrutinize the number of recent inquiries in the most recent 30 to 60 days, to ensure a borrower isn't attempting to acquire too much new credit, too fast.

If lenders or service providers are also concerned about the presence of the second and third possibilities referenced above, then they will request additional verifications of SSNs (with Social Security Cards or a letter from the Social Security Administration) and proof of residential address (with copies of utility bills, mortgage statements or lease agreements).

Finally, if in the most recent two years you've added a personal written statement to your credit reports, then an alert to its presence will appear in this section. As covered in a section in Chapter 5, "Checking and Correcting Your Credit Report," consumer personal statements are oftentimes disregarded and ultimately have no bearing toward the overall scoring or outcome of any credit dispute and will not overturn any decisions based on the plethora of other telling data on the report.

Potentially Negative Items

Some information in this section does its best at confusing and worrying credit report recipients. Some listed items may concern past issues, which have since been resolved. These statements may appear as follows:

- Proportion of balance to available credit limit too high
- Insufficient or lack of credit history
- Previous bankruptcy or foreclosure
- Lien or collection

Potentially Negative Items

Proportion of revolving balances is too high
Previous collection or charge-off

General notes about potentially negative items may appear here. Note that these may be broad in scope and based on previous credit behaviors, and not the most recent credit activity.

Figure 3.7   Sample Report: Potentially Negative Items

Depending on the credit reporting company, the statements vary in vagueness. For example, in the first and second statements, the reporting algorithms may have recognized that a person's credit cards were almost maxed out. But they don't say when and for how long, and this is confusing, to say the least.

When we look at Barry's report (Figure 3.7), we see two of these statements, which means that either currently or at some point Barry may have been utilizing too much of his available credit, too close to being maxed out on his credit cards. And, we know that Barry's had some sort of derogatory item in the form of a collection or charge-off hit his credit report.

Credit and Trade Lines

This is the most data-heavy area of the credit report. All of your debts paid on a monthly basis, known as credit and trade lines, appear here, with all the details relating to that debt. Any closed or paid-in-full accounts will also appear in this section.

Each trade line represents a debt—basically any type of loan or credit card for which you've provided a SSN. Typical trade line items appearing on a credit report are the following:

• Mortgages
• Home equity loans or lines of credit
• Credit cards
• Merchandise cards (tied to retail brands, i.e., Victoria's Secret, Macy's, Home Depot, Best Buy, Rooms-to-Go, you name it)
• Auto loans or leases
• Student loans

You may wonder why your mobile phone bill or utility bills, such as your electric, cable and gas bills, aren't reported as trade lines. Many are shocked when they find out that the items they pay, sometimes with the *greatest* punctuality, are not even reflected on their credit reports.

Utility accounts are not items secured by assets, nor can they accrue like unsecured credit card debt. Rather, they're tied to services or property used for set periods of time, with monthly pay-in-full requirements. You may just think about them a little differently because the consequences of not paying these items are real and with immediate effect. If you don't pay your power bill, your lights go out. If you don't pay your rent, you'll get evicted. Not paying your cell phone bill will get you cut off from the rest of the world.

Here are some examples of items *not* logged on a credit report:

- Apartment rents and leases
- Cell phone bills
- Utilities bills, such as electric, gas, water, and so on
- Insurance bills, such as homeowners, auto, or property insurance

Make no mistake however, that while your payment history on these items isn't reported on a monthly basis, failure to pay them can quickly get you in trouble once the unpaid and outstanding bills are forwarded on to collection agencies. As the Fox Business reporter Dan Rafter said, "While paying these bills on time won't help your credit, falling behind on them can hurt it."[1]

Figures 3.8 and 3.9 show the credit and trade lines in Barry's report.

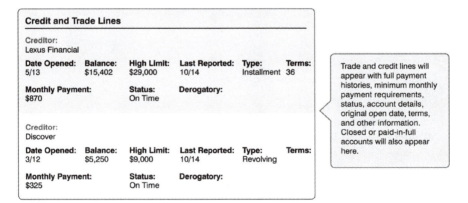

Figure 3.8   Sample Report: Credit and Trade Lines

Credit and Trade Lines

Creditor:
Chase

Date Opened:	Balance:	High Limit:	Last Reported:	Type:	Terms:
4/10	$750	$4,500	9/14	Revolving	

Monthly Payment:		Status:	Derogatory:		
$25		On Time			

Creditor:
Bank of America Visa

Date Opened:	Balance:	High Limit:	Last Reported:	Type:	Terms:
2/08	$2,500	$8,325	10/14	Revolving	

Monthly Payment:		Status:	Derogatory:		
$175		On Time	30 Days, 6/10		

Creditor:
Sallie Mae

Date Opened:	Balance:	High Limit:	Last Reported:	Type:	Terms:
3/06	$39,934	$75,000	10/14	Installment	15

Monthly Payment:		Status:	Derogatory:		
$634		On Time			

Creditor:
MasterCard

Date Opened:	Balance:	High Limit:	Last Reported:	Type:	Terms:
1/06	$4,500	$6,000	10/14	Revolving	

Monthly Payment:		Status:	Derogatory:		
$175		On Time			

CLOSED

Creditor:
ABC Mortgage

Date Opened:	Balance:	High Limit:	Last Reported:	Type:	Terms:
5/06	$189,124	$215,000	12/13	Installment	360

Monthly Payment:		Status:	Derogatory:		
$1,255		PAID IN FULL			

Figure 3.9   Sample Report: Credit and Trade Lines

CREDIT AND TRADE LINES: GETTING GRANULAR

The facts tied to credit and trade lines are of particular interest to lenders. In addition to the name of each creditor, each trade line also includes the following information:

- Date opened: the date the lines of credit or loans were opened
- Balance: the current amount owed
- Original balance/high limit: the amount of the original loan or the high balance on the card for credit card lines
- Last reported: the most recent reporting date that the creditor provided any information about the account
- Type: the type of the debt/account—revolving or installment
- Terms: indicates, usually in months or years, the total length of time of the debt. Applies more to installment debts, rather than revolving debts
- Monthly payment: the minimum monthly required payment due
- Status: indicates whether the debt is current or in delinquent standing
- Derogatory: if a debt is in derogatory standing, indicates whether an outstanding payment is 30-, 60-, 90-, or up to 180-days overdue

Using Barry's report as an example, let's break down a couple of Barry's trade lines (Figure 3.10).

In looking at the Lexus Financial trade line, we can see that Barry first purchased his car back in May 2013 (date opened) for $29,000 (high limit). He secured this debt with an installment loan (type), payable in three years (term). He currently still owes $15,402 (balance) to which he's

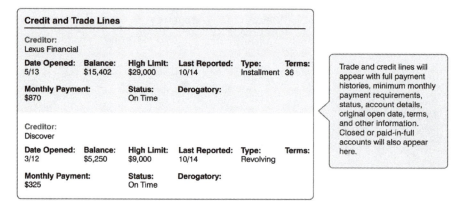

Figure 3.10   Sample Report: Trade Line Detail

making monthly payments of $870 (monthly payment). According to the last reported data, which was in October 2014, he's paying these payments on time (status). Great job, Barry!

On Barry's Discover card, we can see that he's carrying a $5,250 balance out of a $9,000 maximum allowed amount. He's paying the bill on time according to the latest data, and the minimum monthly payment amount he must send to Discover is $325. Of course, sending in the minimum required amount monthly will take Barry much longer to pay off that whole balance of $5,250, which we'll discuss further in Chapter 7, "Managing Debt."

Finally, we see a closed mortgage from ABC Mortgage on Barry's credit report (Figure 3.11). According to the last reported data in December 2013, which was probably when it was paid off, Barry had started this mortgage back in May 2006. The mortgage was originally a 30-year loan, which started at $215,000, and by the time Barry paid it off, likely due to selling the place, the balance was $189,214.

CLOSED

Creditor:
ABC Mortgage

Date Opened:	Balance:	High Limit:	Last Reported:	Type:	Terms:
5/06	$189,124	$215,000	12/13	Installment	360

Monthly Payment:		Status:	Derogatory:
$1,255		PAID IN FULL	

Figure 3.11   Sample Report: Mortgage Detail

What we've just done is what I used to do as a loan officer, and that's go through each trade line to monitor for any derogatory information, as well as look at the total monthly and outstanding debts showing on a credit report. The trade line information paints a very good picture of the report holder's previous as well as current money and credit behaviors. It's also important to understand the two major trade line categories.

TYPES OF TRADE LINES

There are two major types of trade lines: revolving and installment. You may see both on your credit report. The main difference between the two? *Revolving*: These balances are tied to unsecured debt, such as the amounts owed on credit cards. The reason the term is revolving is simply because the debt may come and go, like a revolving door. Some months your unsecured debt is higher; other months it's lower.

If we look at Barry's report, we can see that he has a total of four revolving trade lines, or credit card accounts on his credit report:

Discover, Chase, Bank of America, and MasterCard.

Installment: These balances are usually tied to secured assets or balances to be paid down monthly. Examples of secured assets are houses and cars. Mortgages are secured by the houses to which they're tied, and car loans are obviously secured by the car. Every monthly payment toward these types of debts builds more of your share in ownership, or *equity*, and less of the bank's, until one day, that asset is yours free and clear.

Another installment loan example would be a student loan. Your education secured the loan, and unless the balance is renegotiated, every monthly payment made here will decrease the total balance of the original loan.

In Barry's report, we can see that in addition to his revolving debt, he has installment debt in the form of the Lexus auto loan (as we saw previously) and student loan debt from Sallie Mae.

In the next chapter we discuss how the *types* of trade lines representing the report holder's credit mix ultimately impacts credit scores.

Derogatory Information

Toward the end of the credit report is where most of the negative stuff, such as any judgments, liens, bankruptcies, and collections are listed. Who is owed, how much, and when it was owed will also be listed.

Many times these details are inaccurate and outdated or shouldn't belong on a credit report at all, in which case they'll have to disputed or resolved with the CRAs. Creditors report on a monthly basis and accounts will be noted as current or delinquent. A delinquent status shows as soon as an account goes beyond 30-days late. After 180 days the creditor may forward an outstanding debt on to a collection agency.

According to Barry's report (Figure 3.12), looks like he had a collection filed against him by Con Edison, his previous electric provider. But it also

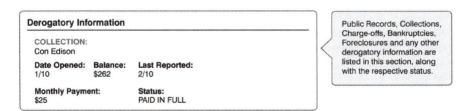

Figure 3.12   Sample Report: Derogatory Info

looks like it was old (from January 2010) and not for too much money ($262), and that he paid it shortly after it was filed, in February 2010.

Inquiries

Finally, credit reports list any inquiry activity made on the borrowers' behalf usually within the most recent six months. An inquiry is logged on a credit report anytime new loans and services are requested, for example, a new credit card application or mortgage or loan prequalification. It is also possible to see inquiries tied to credit card prequalification offers, or utility company credit checks.

Looks like Barry's had four since 2012, and they were either inquiries for new credit (Capital One, Best Rate Mortgage, Best Buy) or services (Verizon Wireless) (Figure 3.13).

Personal Statements

As part of FACTA, CRAs can now accept 100-word personal statements attached to credit files. While this may be helpful in explaining your situation or reasons for any specific derogatory activity on accounts, keep in mind that this does nothing to help with credit scores. Credit-scoring algorithms don't read these statements. Lenders don't read these statements, either, which is why you want to do your best at ensuring the actual data is as accurate as possible.

Inquiries		
Capital One	3/2014	
Best Rate Mortgage Company	1/2014	
Best Buy	1/2013	
Verizon Wireless	10/2012	

A list of the most recent requests for your credit history. Some reports may provide a more thorough list that separates inquires initiated by you, or by creditors who are screening to make credit offers.

Figure 3.13   Sample Report: Credit Inquiries

Personal Statements
CONSUMER STATEMENT: PLEASE CONTACT ME AT 212-555-5555 FOR ANY NEW CREDIT ACCOUNT REQUESTS.

Any personal statements provided to creditors to prevent consumer fraud, or any explanation on facts or conditions of any items on the credit report.

Figure 3.14   Sample Report: Personal Statements

In Barry's report, he requested to be contacted for new credit applications; this or a fraud alert could alert lenders to verify an applicant's information (Figure 3.14).

Personal History and Verification Data

Some credit reports will also list a consumer's residential history and name variations. Lenders may ask that credit applicants verify addresses, and any previous names or aliases used. They may also compare this data alongside an applicant's verification documents such as a driver's license, passport, social security card, or utility statements showing current addresses.

Putting It All Together

Remember the name mismatch in Barry's file? We can link it to this section as well. Here's where we do a bit of detective work to find out why this name variation exists.

Anytime new credit applications are filed, the personal information—exactly as it was entered to pull the report—is logged. If the data entered to pull credit contains typos, these are recorded. A log of Barry's name as "Baron" was logged in October 2012 (Figure 3.15). Why? We can look at the inquiries section and link a Verizon Wireless credit with this date.

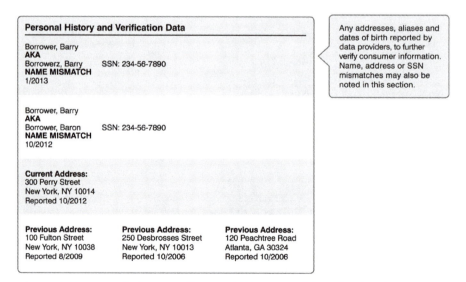

Figure 3.15   Sample Report: Personal History and Verification Data

Perhaps this was a clerical error on the Verizon data entrant's part. Regardless, if Barry were to apply for a new mortgage loan tomorrow, the lender would likely see these variations and ask to see Barry's verification documents to confirm (1) he is who he says he is and (2) the correct spelling of his name compared to what's on his file.

Now that you've got a good understanding of the components of a credit report, let's get your credit reports and scores.

GETTING YOUR CREDIT REPORTS

We're ready. Let's get your credit report and scores. We know there are a gazillion providers, but which is best? There are many options—more than you can count when it comes to getting a credit report.

But not all credit reporting companies are made equal. For example, some provide free reports; yet they don't offer credit scores. And many companies require some sort of add-on monthly credit monitoring subscription before they will reveal your scores. The other main difference is the perplexing question of which score actually matters.

Remember our jeans analogy from Chapter 1? Keep in mind that you can get CRA jeans from everywhere, but you may only want those with that special FICO thread. But guess what? You could also buy the next best thing, a designer look-alike, or even be handed a completely free pair that is surprisingly similar, and that might be enough.

Your Options: Free vs. Paid, Scores vs. No Scores

Our main goal is to get all three of your credit reports and scores, for the least amount of money as possible. How you go about it is whether you prefer convenience to cost and whether you definitely want your FICO scores or will settle for something similar.

My recommendation: Complete step 1. Then choose an option in either step 2 or step 3.

By completing step 1 and step 2, you'll have your complete individual CRA reports and a paid, streamlined tri-merge report with all three credit scores, including your FICO scores.

By completing step 1 and step 3, you'll have your complete individual CRA reports and free separate reports with scores. These may not be your FICO scores, but will give you a very good idea of where you stand.

Step 1: Free Annual Credit Reports from the CRAs

Why would I recommend ordering these free single reports sans score? Because you want to know what each CRA is reporting about you.

Personally, I'd be interested to see how my information varies from CRA to CRA, though in most cases they are very similar. If you do have a negative item on your credit report, you'll want to know the source.

The major CRAs offer you a free credit report every year because they're required to do so under the Fair Credit Reporting Act and specifically the Fair and Accurate Credit Transactions Act. You can order them easily online with one form at www.annualcreditreport.com. You can also submit a request in writing by filling out the form available directly from the site or at www.tccbonline.com. Once you order your reports, they arrive within 15 days. You will receive separate reports, one from each CRA. *Remember that these free reports only disclose credit history and not scores.*

You may think, "Why would I request anything by snail mail when I can get it instantaneously online?" Yes, all of us live in an on-demand digital age, but remember that when ordering or buying anything online, you become subject to any seller's or provider's terms and conditions, arbitration agreements, and limitations on liability. I'm not saying to not order the reports online, but I just want you to be aware of literature and opinions that have suggested otherwise.

I repeat this later, in Chapter 5, where I discuss the process of disputing inaccurate credit items. If you end up having to dispute or request any removal of negative and inaccurate information, it's recommended to *do it in writing and not online.* Personally, I have always requested credit reports and made disputes in writing.

Once you've ordered your free credit reports, you'll want to order reports that actually disclose your credit scores.

You need an idea of each individual CRA's score because these are used to determine your creditworthiness. And since each of the three CRAs claim they have spent lots of time and money on the formulaic algorithms that go into calculating your scores, they're not offering them for free.

Even corporations who must pull full credit reports for business processes—for example industries requiring credit information such as mortgage lending or insurance—must pay for credit score data.

Instead of three separate reports, there are options for you to purchase all three CRA reports with scores merged into one, also known as a tri-merge report. This consolidates the paperwork and makes it easier to just have one file from which to reference all the reports. But while it may be convenient to seek out this one-stop shop credit report with the trifecta of data you seek, the CRAs don't offer it for free, nor cheap. There are costs involved in obtaining this data—it just depends on your personal preference for convenience over cost and vice versa.

So while the reports at www.annualcreditreport.com may be a great way to check on the accuracy of your personal credit history on file with the majors, the scores also matter, especially if you're planning on a major purchase such as a car or house.

Rather than overwhelm you with every major credit reporting company under the sun, here's how you can order your credit report and scores from the traditional major CRAs and one solid alternative. The direct-from-CRA reports are going to give you the Beacon, FICO, and Empirica scores you often hear about. As of the writing of this book, the three CRAs were offering the following products and services to obtain a tri-merge credit report.

One note: if you're currently in the process of getting a preapproval for a mortgage or car loan, and your loan officer or representative has already pulled a copy of your credit report, *ask for a copy*. What's the worst that could happen? They say no. Your loan representative probably won't have a problem with it unless the company prevents the person from doing so. When I was a loan officer, I was happy to include a copy of my clients' credit reports along with their loan application. And even if they didn't go as far as a loan application, if they asked for a copy of their credit report, I'd give them a copy for free. *Now, pick from step 2 (Paid tri-merge reports with scores from the CRAs) or step 3 (Free single reports with scores).*

Step 2: Paid Tri-Merge Reports with Scores from the Credit Reporting Agencies

You can choose to order a tri-merge report with scores directly from Equifax or Experian. As of this writing, TransUnion did not offer a tri-merge report, only its own single score report. Any links listed below are also accessible from www.tccbonline.com.

EQUIFAX (BEACON)

Equifax offers a single consolidated tri-merge report with scores and data from all three CRAs, merged into one. This may be the simplest option in obtaining a tri-merge report with all three scores.

Link: www.equifax.com/credit-bureau-report

The cost of the tri-merge report and scores is $39.95.

Equifax also offers a complete report pack, which allows three credit pulls within a three-month period, but I can't imagine why anyone would want this service, especially not with today's plethora of free credit tools and apps (discussed further in this section) that can help monitor your scores and activity for free. It's expensive, too!

Link: www.equifax.com/credit-report-pack/.

The cost of the complete report pack (three credit pulls in three months) is $99.95.

Experian (FICO)

Experian offers a premium service for just its own score (which you can bypass) and go straight to their tri-merge report, which is the same cost as Equifax's tri-merge report. If for some reason you are interested in the single score, it is only available for seven days, after which time you'll be charged $19.95 per month for a subscription program which includes daily credit monitoring, resolution support, and access to an Experian credit hotline.

Link: www.experian.com/consumer-products/credit-score.html

The cost of the tri-merge report and scores is $39.95.

The cost of a single score is $1 for seven days, $19.95 monthly thereafter.

The statistics aren't available regarding how many orders the CRAs get for their products. I think part of the reason why most people don't care to order their personal credit reports directly from the CRAs is the annoyance factor of being looped into sneaky subscriptions of products they don't need; I really detest having to enter my credit card information for anything that's promised as free or even as low as $1 and then having to *remind myself* to go back and cancel.

There is a term for this kind of marketing tactic that involves the looping-in of customers and waiting out noncancellation of services, and those are called free-to-paid grey charges. Apparently it's such a successful tactic that it racks up roughly $6 billion in American cardholder revenues every year.[2] Remember that CRAs are also in the business to collect and report consumer data, which I would believe is the bulk of their business. They sell these consumer products and monitoring as additional revenue streams.

Paid Tri-Merge Reports with Scores from Other Sources

Alternatively, choose from one of the non-CRA sources below to obtain tri-merge reports.

The site myfico.com is the consumer arm of FICO and provides your FICO scores from the three CRAs for $19.95. This is a bare-bones report that simply lists scores as well as factors affecting your score also known as the Potentially Negative Items in Barry Borrower's sample credit report, but it doesn't provide comprehensive full reports per CRA at this price.

For the full CRA reports and their FICO scores in a side-by-side comparison, you'll have to cough up $59.85.

Now don't fret. Just because FICO is the most recognized and used among the industry doesn't mean that other credit report and score providers won't provide a solid idea of where you stand for credit cleanup, repair, monitoring, and preparing for major purchases. FICO is simply the model from which the CRAs have based their own scoring models.

The cost is $19.95 for scores only, and $58.95 for full reports and scores.

Creditscore.com does offer tri-merge reports and scores for less than the major CRAs, at $12.95 and *only* if you continue with credit monitoring services at this cost on a monthly basis. There is no way to obtain a onetime report from creditscore.com for a flat fee. Instead, you *must* sign up for their credit monitoring service before you can view your reports.

You are, however, allowed to cancel your monitoring membership at any time, so if you're willing to pay up front for one month's membership, then you can do so to obtain your credit scores and reports and then cancel the membership—just remember to cancel, otherwise you will be lumped in with the national statistic of companies that make money from the grey charges mentioned earlier. It's an extra step, but you'll be able to get the information you need quickly.

According to Cliff Brody, a self-professed credit report expert at reviews.com, creditscore.com "features a ScoreTracker tool, which sends e-mail alerts every time your credit score goes up or down. This, along with detailed information about the factors that affect your score, helps you make informed financial decisions and raise your credit score over time."

ScoreTracker is included in the creditscore.com credit monitoring service, so it doesn't cost extra and might be just what you need to reach a credit score goal. Another important note is that creditscore.com doesn't provide FICO scores, but you should still be able to get a fairly accurate estimate of where you stand.[3]

In creditscore.com's score center, there is an Estimate Your Score page where you can see how certain actions will impact your credit score. Actions like opening a new account, missing a payment, and applying for a new credit card or making a loan application can impact your score in a big way, and this tool enables you to see just how significant that impact will be.

The monthly cost is $12.95.

As I recall, myfico.com was the first to offer a credit simulator tool, which shows how certain activities, like paying down debt or opening new credit, can impact credit scores. Since then, similar tools have now been enhanced, improved and continue to be wildly popular with consumers. These free tools are very welcome because they help demystify the weights and balances of how credit is scored. More is discussed on this topic in Chapter 6, "Improving Your Credit Score."

Step 3: Free Single Reports with Scores

Now that we've seen some of the offers out there for tri-merge reports, let's discover free ways to obtain your scores, piecemeal.

Luckily for all of us, technology and innovation have sprung a breed of companies that are determined to lift the veil over our eyes regarding credit reporting and scoring. And with them, you do feel as if they've placed the consumer and a consumer's right-to-knowledge, first. They're even providing your valuable score data for less money, and even for *free*.

Business Insider said it best: "For some reason, the geniuses of credit reporting decided it'd be a good idea to offer the physical report for free once a year and dangle the actual score itself in front of us like a juicy carrot. If you want to find out your actual credit *score* you usually have to pay and endure a barrage of ads for all sorts of different credit monitoring products in the meantime."[4]

While the companies referenced later may not offer a standard tri-merge report, they do offer a single score based on a major CRA's score and a ton of other feature-packed tools for credit management, such as credit score simulators, basic credit monitoring, and identity theft services.

While mixing and matching your reports and scores might be more of a hunter-gatherer approach, if you would prefer to obtain your credit reports and scores for free (and who wouldn't) by collecting them from multiple sources, then give these a try. The biggest difference between the scores offered by these sites depends on which credit reporting agency data they are based. Also remember, as mentioned earlier, that while they aren't the major CRAs' FICO scores, they will each give you a pretty good idea of where you stand.

Credit Sesame (creditsesame.com)

A consumer favorite, Credit Sesame lets you get your Experian score, totally free, without requiring you to provide any credit card information

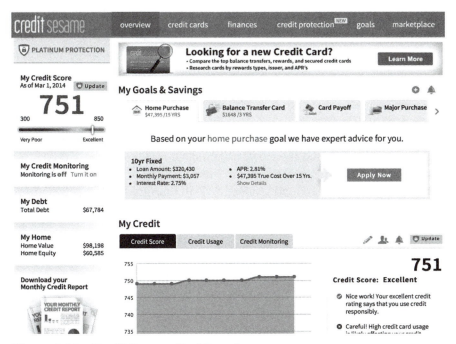

Figure 3.16   Credit Sesame Dashboard

and without subscribing to any services. It also has a free credit monitoring service that alerts you of any changes or new activity to your credit report.

The company has been around since launching as a tech startup in private beta at TechCrunch Disrupt in 2010.[5] As of this writing, Credit Sesame analyzes roughly $35 billion in registered users' loans on a daily basis for potential consumer savings.

Free Experian Score: In addition to providing a free Experian score, its free web-based tool helps you manage your credit and recommends money-saving options on loans that it deems are a good fit for you. Figure 3.16 shows what their overview page looks like when you log in.

The highly reviewed free app for both Apple and Android operating systems also allows users to obtain scores and access many of the features from the full web experience (Figure 3.17).

Credit Sesame's proprietary analysis model starts the minute clients create their profiles based on their Experian credit profiles. The engines under the hood then analyze users' current loans (including mortgage, credit card, auto loan, and student loan accounts) and look for alternative loans that will help that client save money.

Prescreened Opportunities: The mortgage and refinance loans that Credit Sesame recommends to users are completely unique and based on each individual user's credit file. The software looks at factors such as estimated home value and considers any financial goals users set up upon registration. Because it houses a consumer's loans and credit information all in one place, it provides a pretty solid picture of only that consumer's overall financial situation.

When I spoke with Credit Sesame's Chief Marketing Officer Olivier Lemaignen, he stressed the power behind the analytics, the engineering behind the marketing, which is continuously under development under lead scientist Ken Singleton, also a professor in finance at Stanford

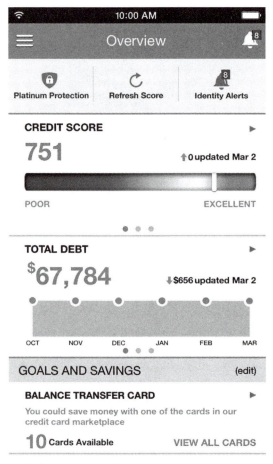

Figure 3.17   Credit Sesame Mobile App

University Graduate School of Business. He indicated that the company actually started as a business-to-business engine, originally intending its algorithmic recommendations for use by professional financial advisors when they were trying to advise clients on better managing personal debt.

The data modeling is indeed impressive. Olivier stressed that it is what truly differentiates Credit Sesame from competitors in the field, in that their recommendations are already matched with the data pulled from your Experian profile. "Oftentimes, users may think that our recommendations are tied to loans or offers with higher rates. But it's because our analytics are so smart and have already looked at your payment capabilities based on your complete credit and debt picture—like how much you're likely to pay or save—and we'll already know whether you won't be able to qualify for those teaser rates on other sites, which are usually reserved only for those with perfect credit." Note the offer at the bottom of the overview in app version.

Olivier also stated, "You'll eventually get offered rates that are similar to what our system recommended in the first place, because we've done the pre-screening and analyzing beforehand for you." But rest assured, he clarified, because they, unlike the CRAs, do not reveal any of their users' personal financial records to advertisers. They serve as the middleman in the process of filtering and recommending of services.

Goals: You can also set savings goals which the system will use to start looking for products and offers that may benefit you. There's no guarantee that you will qualify for all the offers, since Credit Sesame's recommendations are based only on behaviors and actual payment history. Let's say you reach a point where you no longer require its services—say, you've met your credit and savings goals. Once you delete your account, your data and history are completely wiped from their systems—nothing lingers so you don't have to worry about any personal and private information hanging out in their servers. "Once you delete your account, you delete your history. You're wiped from our system," Olivier stated, which is pretty reassuring considering that the CRAs are already collecting, keeping, and sharing as much data on you as possible and will continue doing so until the end of time. Figure 3.18 shows what the Goals tool looks like on the web.

As of this writing Credit Sesame will have also launched its Advanced Credit feature, which at $9.95 per month will allow an instantaneous credit score refresh, for as many times as you want and also includes a full credit report on a monthly basis. This service may be useful for those who are anticipating major score changes due to credit disputes, new credit, or debt pay down.

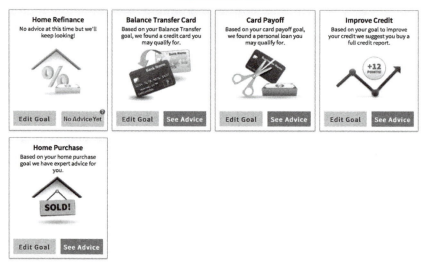

Do More With Your Score!

Select your financial goals to get our unbiased advice to save money and improve your score.

Your Selected Goals

Home Refinance
No advice at this time but we'll keep looking!
Edit Goal   No Advice Yet

Balance Transfer Card
Based on your Balance Transfer goal, we found a credit card you may qualify for.
Edit Goal   See Advice

Card Payoff
Based on your card payoff goal, we found a personal loan you may qualify for.
Edit Goal   See Advice

Improve Credit
Based on your goal to improve your credit we suggest you buy a full credit report.
Edit Goal   See Advice

Home Purchase
Based on your home purchase goal we have expert advice for you.
Edit Goal   See Advice

Add More Goals Below

| Credit | Home | Auto | Credit Cards | Personal Loan | 0% Financing |

Figure 3.18   Credit Sesame "Goals"

Identity Monitoring: Credit Sesame already offers a highly popular Identity Protection service at $9.95 per month, which will alert you in all cases of new applications for credit, that is, the enquiries that can negatively impact credit scores, further discussed in Chapter 4, "What Credit Scores Like and Don't Like."

Finally, there's a platinum plan at $14.95 per month, which includes advanced credit and a cool SSN geolocator feature, which can find and alert you wherever your SSN is used for any new credit inquiries. This essentially makes Credit Sesame the only one-stop shop where your credit information, financial products, and identity protection are all in one place. It allows you to limit the number of companies with whom you share your most valuable personal information (your SSN), and Credit Sesame has bank-level security to keep your information safe.

Education: Credit Sesame also has a breadth of consumer-focused content on its blog. "We invest a lot of time writing original content to put education at the forefront. We are the most interviewed, quoted, Reddit-ed, wide-variety, not product-based, unbiased education center for consumers," Olivier said. And the best part? All of the education materials, like its basic score service, are free!

CREDIT KARMA (CREDITKARMA.COM)

Unlike Credit Sesame, Credit Karma provides a score based on TransUnion data. And, they also do this for free with no credit card and no hidden costs or obligations. They market this as being "good karma indeed"!

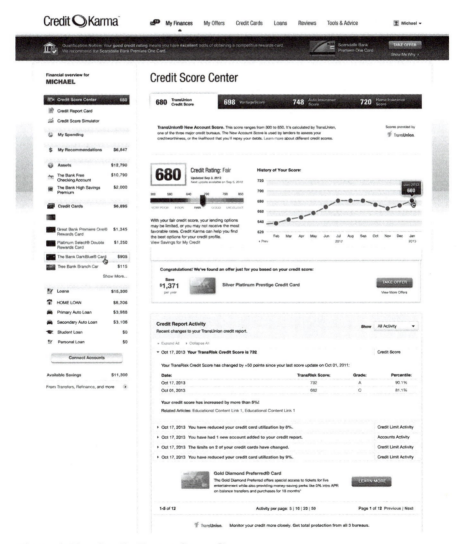

Figure 3.19   Credit Karma Score Center

Credit Karma was founded in 2007 on the idea that consumers should have free access to their credit and financial data. The company also provides account and transactions monitoring, savings recommendations, consumer reviews, and advice from its more than 30 million other members. Figure 3.19 shows what the dashboard looks like when you log in.

Some of Credit Karma's main product features include the following:

Free Transunion Score: You'll receive your free credit score along with a credit report card, which gives you a letter grade on each of the most important factors that go into calculating your score. You get a transparent, easy-to-understand picture of your credit health.

Free Credit Monitoring: Credit Karma will send you an e-mail alert whenever something important changes in your TransUnion credit report. This will help you monitor your credit report for accuracy and quickly catch fraudulent activity.

Financial Account Monitoring: By connecting your banking, savings, credit card, and loan accounts to Credit Karma, you can keep tabs on your balances and transactions daily. They'll alert you of any unusual account activity and see where you're spending the most.

Opportunities to Save: Credit Karma makes personalized recommendations based on your credit and financial profile. You can also use their vast consumer shopping database by comparing interest rates on credit cards and loans.

Mobile: Credit Karma also has a highly rated app for iPhone and Android, and you can check your credit score and receive credit monitoring alerts from the app, anywhere. Figure 3.20 shows what the app's main dashboard looks like.

According to Credit Karma, its distinct goal is to always offer its services and educational resources for free to consumers. There are no trial subscriptions and no premium access accounts.

How Do They Make Money?

You may wonder how companies who are offering free scores make money. They are of course businesses as well, and they make money from credit company advertising and when their users take them up on their loan, credit card, and savings recommendations.

Ultimately, they act like reverse lead-generation systems for creditors and are doing the heavy lifting for financial institutions that rely on them for prescreening customers. Aside from that, they do offer a fantastic service for consumers who simply want to know where they stand credit-wise.

Figure 3.20   Credit Karma Mobile App

ONE FINAL MENTION

FICO Score Open Access: In early 2014, a program called FICO Score Open Access was created, and it allows credit card companies to provide free FICO scores to their customers, giving them access to view the same scores that lenders use to evaluate their accounts.

If you'll recall, the Discover card was heavily marketing this program in television advertisements earlier this year.

Lenders may also offer clients additional free (and likely promotional) material from FICO, such as a personalized statement that outlines significant factors affecting your score. Clients can access scores through online accounts with the lender, on paper statements, or on mobile devices.

Keep in mind, this version of the FICO score that your credit card company reveals may not be the same one that, say, your auto or mortgage lender uses, but it's going to be pretty close.

As of this writing only a few creditors were participating: Discover, Barclaycard US, and First Bankcard (which is the credit card division of the First National Bank of Omaha).

FOUR

The Credit Score

Now that you've obtained your scores, no matter which method you used to gather them, they *should* all be pretty similar based on your overall credit history. If your score is excellent with one bureau, it *should* be reflected this way among the others.

Another point: within each company's reports there may be additional charts, codes, and groupings of numbers specific only to that company. Don't pay too much information to these, but instead focus your attention on the general risk level of your credit score: good to bad, or high to low.

When FICO released information about its scoring models in 2003, it lifted the lid on what factors were used to determine credit score ranges. As mentioned before, the major CRAs now use this model and tweak it further to fit within their proprietary systems.

So how is credit scored? Let's take a look.

ANATOMY OF A SCORE

According to Figure 4.1, FICO's model is based on the following factors:

Payment History = 35 Percent

Paying your bills and debts on time has the most significant impact on your credit score and is also the easiest way to start improving your score.

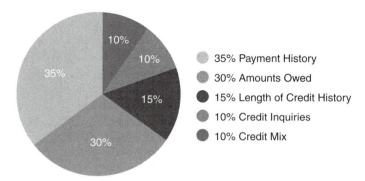

Figure 4.1   Credit Mix

The more recent your late payments, the more negatively it impacts your score. This is because late payments turn into collections, charge-offs, and judgments, and these factors also have a significant negative impact on your overall score.

Amounts Owed = 30 Percent

Another fancy name for this simple concept has cropped up in recent years, called the credit utilization rate. But simply speaking, this factor counts the total amount of credit *used* versus the total amount of credit *available*. If you're close to being maxed out on your credit cards, then you would have a *high* utilization rate as opposed to someone who carries little to no credit card debt, and has *low* utilization.

Length of Credit History = 15 Percent

This factor takes into consideration how long you've established your credit history across various accounts. If you've had a long credit history, perhaps with various types of credit over a period of time, then this would be more favorable than if you carried very little or recent credit. The older your overall credit history, the better. Parents with longer credit history would fare better in this area than children with more recent credit history or no credit history at all.

Credit Inquiries = 10 Percent

This factor is determined by the number of inquiries, or requests for new credit, that appear on your credit history within the most recent six to 12 month period.

Credit Mix = 10 Percent

Your credit mix looks at the combination of revolving and installment debt, first discussed in Chapter 3, "The Credit Report." A mix of auto loans, credit cards, and mortgages would weigh more positively than a concentration of unsecured debt from credit cards alone.

While these are the basic components of the credit score, keep in mind that each CRA tweaks this formula so that it fits their unique models, which is why when you pull the tri-merge report, you should get three *similar* but not *identical* scores.

Myfico.com says, "Each of the three credit reporting agencies probably has different information about you, and that means your scores will also be different. If your information is identical at all three credit reporting agencies, your (FICO) scores should be pretty close."[1]

It's also a fact that the credit scores purchased by consumers are not the same scores used by companies, lenders, and insurers. This is why it's a good idea to simply know where you stand, rather than fixate on the score. Most credit reports these days will also often have an indicator to show you your general risk level.

The Consumer Financial Protection Bureau is aware of the differences between credit scores that consumers receive versus the scores that maybe used among industries such as mortgage or insurance.

According to the CFPB,

> To determine if score variations would lead to meaningful differences between the consumers' and lenders' assessment of credit quality, the [Analysis of Differences between Consumer- and Creditor-Purchased Credit Scores] study divided scores into four credit-quality categories.
>
> The study found that different scoring models would place consumers in the same credit-quality category 73–80 percent of the time. Different scoring models would place consumers in credit-quality categories that are off by one category 19–24 percent of the time. And from 1 to 3 percent of consumers would be placed in categories that were two or more categories apart.[2]

Which means that the consumer-scoring models, or the excellent, good, fair, or poor categories used to label the majority of credit scores purchased or accessed by consumers, is similar (at roughly 80 percent) to what those industries are seeing when they make their credit decisions. Again, if your score is within good to excellent credit tiers on one report, it should be very similar on others.

So what are the credit tiers?

Excellent = 750
Good   = 700–749
Average   = 650–699
Bad   = 500–640
Poor   = below 500

According to FICO's Risk of Default calculations, the likelihood of a person with over 750 scores making late payments is less than 2 percent; however, if you have a credit score in the range of 600–649, FICO estimates you may pay bills late roughly 31 percent of the time.[3]

And if you were wondering where most Americans stand, the median credit score in the United States since 2011 has been 711.[4]

Take a look at Figure 4.2, which is another interesting data table from myfico.com, and shows that the majority of people in the United States have scores above 700. Notice how, from October 2007 through October 2013, that the percentage of most people with scores over 800 hasn't changed. What *has* changed over the years is the number of people who have fallen out of the 750–799 category and into the score ranges of 550–599, 600–659 (the spread with the most growth during this time period), and 700–749.

This could be attributed to the credit crisis' aftermath since 2007. Perhaps people used more credit cards as backups for emergencies during difficult times. As lending tightened, they may also have turned to unsecured credit card debt for added liquidity. Unemployment may also have prevented many from paying bills on time, impacting their credit scores.

In mortgage lending, if the other components of your qualifying criteria in the form of income and assets look solid, then a credit score above 720 should open up most loan programs to you. If your score is 760 and above, then that will weigh heavily in your favor, especially considering that most loan underwriting approvals are run through automated systems first and place a lot of emphasis on the middle credit score of the three.

If you're also interested in credit-scoring by state, there is a fantastic interactive credit map at governing.com, also accessible from tccbonline.com. In a nutshell, the top five U.S. states with the best average Experian credit scores are:

Minnesota: 718
North Dakota: 715

FICO* Score Distribution

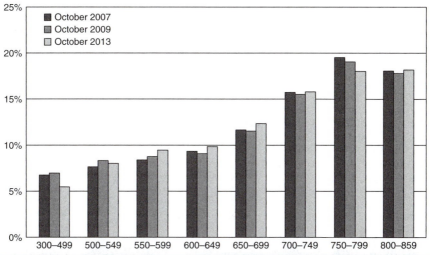

PERCENT OF POPULATION									
FICO* 8 Score	October 2005	October 2006	October 2007	October 2008	October 2009	October 2010	October 2011	October 2012	October 2013
300–499	6.6	6.5	7.1	7.2	7.3	6.9	6.3	6.0	5.8
500–549	8.0	8.0	8.0	8.2	8.7	9.0	8.7	8.5	8.4
550–599	9.0	8.8	8.7	8.7	9.1	9.6	9.9	9.9	9.8
600–649	10.2	10.2	9.7	9.6	9.5	9.5	9.8	10.1	10.2
650–699	12.8	12.5	12.1	12.0	11.9	11.9	12.1	12.2	12.7
700–749	16.4	16.3	16.2	16.0	15.9	15.7	15.5	16.2	16.3
750–799	20.1	19.8	19.8	19.6	19.4	19.5	19.6	18.8	18.4
800–859	16.9	17.9	18.4	18.7	18.2	17.9	18.1	18.4	18.6
TOTAL*	100	100	100	100	100	100	100	100	100

*All columns may not add up to 100.0% due to rounding.
FICO™ Banking Analytics Blog. © 2014 Fair Isaac Corporation.

Figure 4.2   FICO Score Distribution

South Dakota: 712
Vermont: 712
New Hampshire: 711

This means that those living in the Midwest and New England areas are generally following the mold when it comes to credit management. Not bad.

Let's now a take deeper look at what specifically drives the inner components behind each credit-scoring factor.

WHAT SCORES LIKE AND DON'T LIKE

Now that we have an idea of what factors most impact a credit score, let's do a deeper dive behind each component. Knowing the underlying methodology behind each component and how they all relate to each other is the knowledge that will give you power to raise your credit score.

Payment History: Pay Your Bills on Time (35 Percent of Credit Score)

You are most rewarded on your credit score for paying all of your bills *on time*. Let me stress this: *pay your bills on time*. Late bill payments also have the most adverse impact on your score. Your ability to make timely payments says a lot about personal financial responsibility and is crucial to how lenders and companies will determine your eligibility for the loans and services you need.

Within payment history are a number of subfactors of which you should be aware:

Recent Late Payments Hit Scores Hardest: The most recent 12 months of payment history are most crucial to credit scores. A single 30-day late payment on any bill can lower scores by as much as 15 to 40 points, and missing payments for all of your bills in the same month can cause a score to tank by 150 points or more![5] Those 150 points are easy to lose and much harder to gain back.

The Greater the Lateness, the Worse the Damage: Once your bills go unpaid past the 30-day mark, and become 60-, 90-, and 180-days late, these consecutive late payments will hurt your score exponentially. What this means is the more and more you fall behind, the more your credit score is dinged. The late payments after the initial 30-days incrementally drive your score downward.

Higher Scores Take a Greater Hit: Recent lateness takes more points off excellent than average or bad scores. "For example, for someone with a score over 800, one 30-day late payment can reduce a score by 100 points, whereas someone with a score of 650 may see a change of only 25 points for the same late bill payment."[6]

Chronically Late Payments Should Be Avoided: Paying late on one bill doesn't look as bad as paying late on all of your bills. Don't allow late bill payments to become a frequency.

Collections, Bankruptcies, Liens, and Judgments: These derogatory items remain on credit scores for up to 10 years. For outstanding collections, the more recent they are, the worse. Very old collection accounts don't hurt scores as much, and eventually, bankruptcies, liens and judgments (if satisfied accordingly) should eventually come off credit reports.

Amounts Owed: Keep Your Balances within Reason (30 Percent of Credit Score)

The balances owed, in proportion to the total credit available has the second greatest impact toward your score. Ideally, you should make an effort to keep your balances as close to or as low as possible compared to the maximum amount allowed.

Cutoffs for Consideration

Credit utilization is ranked in tiers; so understanding the cutoffs for each tier is to your advantage.

Credit utilization tiers based on percentages:

0–19 percent
20–39 percent
40–59 percent
60–79 percent
80–99 percent
100 percent

Each increasing tier harms a score the same as the previous (e.g., if a balance goes from 39 to 40 percent, it will impact the score the same as it would going from 79 to 80 percent). Keep your balances on your revolving accounts (unsecured credit card debt) below 40 percent of the credit limit, and try to never exceed that amount, unless for emergency funds.

It's best to try keeping balances less than 19 percent, which as you can see has the same weight as carrying only 1 percent of the total amount.

Unsecured Debt Is a Killer

In the scoring process, FICO usually looks at the revolving (unsecured credit card) account that is charged closest to its max limit and weighs the heaviest. It then looks at other revolving accounts, and then installment loan balances, and considers the total amounts owed versus the maximum debt available.

A note about equity lines of credit: If you opened a home equity line of credit (HELOC) recently, know that these are sometimes counted as revolving debt, instead of being counted as secured debt collateralized by property. Unlike a second mortgage, which resembles a standard mortgage because it is an installment loan with a fixed starting balance and term, the balances on equity lines of credit can go up or down. The reason for this? There is support to show that FICO considers low-balance HELOCs, say up to $10,000, to be revolving accounts, whereas those with higher limits say, upward of $30,000, are treated as second mortgages.[7] While we can't be sure as to the exact balance tiers, it seems to be the *amount* of the total credit line that deems whether it is revolving or installment debt.

Small Balances Are Better than Zero Balances

Before you pay all your credit cards off and never touch them again, hold on a minute. While you may think that having zero balances is a sure-fire strategy for an excellent credit score, the truth is that this tactic doesn't help a score at all. Only responsible usage of credit—charging and keeping low balances and/or paying for them in full monthly—boosts scores. Utilizing your available credit prudently is good for credit scores.

Length of Credit History (15 Percent of Credit Score)

The third most significant component of credit-scoring is the length of your *overall* credit history as well as the *age* of your individual accounts. If you have a good, longstanding credit mix (discussed next), then you'll want to keep these accounts open for as long you can. Here, mortgages, student loans, and anything that requires a long time to pay off will usually help, as well as credit cards that were opened a long time ago and remain open.

Having zero or no credit history will negatively impact you, so the only way to build credit is to use it wisely over time.

Credit Mix (10 Percent of Credit Score)

When it comes to credit, there is such a thing as good or bad credit. It looks like the best mix is a combination of secured and unsecured debt. The mix of installment and well-managed revolving debt do a lot of good to a credit score. This would look like a mix of a mortgage, auto loan or student loan, and credit cards. For perspective: "The average American has 13 credit accounts showing on their credit report, including 9 credit cards and 4 installment loans," according to Fair Isaac.

I also recently learned that FICO picks up on the quality of a debt holder and can recognize when lenders or creditors are bona fide banks, or just finance companies. Consider this: any merchant or retailers that are always offering same-as-cash deals for a certain period of time (90 days, six months, the first year, and so on) are typically backed by finance companies, not banks like Chase or Bank of America or lenders like Toyota Motor Credit, or standard creditors like American Express, Visa, or MasterCard. FICO picks up on the quality of the credit for which you've qualified, so keep it in mind before you open any new credit. This leads to inquiries.

Inquiries (10 Percent of Credit Score)

Inquiries are logged when any new applications for credit are submitted. Inquiries that result in opening a lot of new accounts in a short period of time can ding your credit score, especially when you have an overall shorter length of credit history.

Mortgage Rate Shopping Is Not Penalized

A discrepancy exists here however, and this is when you are getting preapproved for a mortgage. When you are rate shopping, you can have multiple inquiries up to a 14-day period, and you will only be penalized for one. Also, know that FICO is based on activity for the prior 30 days, so your scores should not be fluctuating while you are rate shopping.

Otherwise, each individual inquiry—up to 10 inquiries—can hurt your credit score by as much as five to 30 points.

Not All Inquiries Are Made Equal

A "soft" pull will not hurt your credit score. Examples of soft credit pulls include those for the following purposes:

1. Ordering a personal credit report
2. Setting up utilities (e.g., your water, electric, gas, and cable services)
3. Receiving prescreened or preapproved credit card solicitations and offers
4. Prescreening for employment purposes
5. Credit monitoring

An important note about item no. 2: while you may be prescreened or pre-approved for a new credit card, understand that once you take up the offer, you will be required to release the information that is required for a hard pull, which is what can ding your credit.

Opt-Out: It's Your Right

If you don't want creditors and banks prescreening your credit without your knowledge and don't want solicitations for credit card and/or loan offers, then dial the National Opt-Out hotline or submit your request via the online opt-out form. Creditors and financial institutions prescreen consumer credit records for the purposes of shortlisting a target group to send prescreened credit card offers. If you've got credit, then your name is already on a marketing list, and you're likely being checked for your credit usage and total credit utilization. If you've got excellent credit because you carry very little credit card debt, you may be solicited for credit cards with the best or lowest annual percentage rates (APRs). Creditors can also see if you're carrying a lot of consumer debt, and you may then be shortlisted for a credit card that offers a low or 0 percent interest rate on transferred balances. More on managing debt is mentioned later in Chapter 7, under Debt Management Tips.

But what if you don't want to receive prescreened credit offers? If you're deluged with these offers and want them to stop, you have the right to opt out. Here's the information from the Federal Trade Commission and on the related ftc.gov webpage.[8]

You can opt out of receiving them for five years or opt out of receiving them permanently.

To opt out for five years: Call toll-free *opt-out* (1-888-567-8688) or visit optoutprescreen.com.

To opt out permanently: You may begin the permanent opt-out process online at optoutprescreen.com. To complete your request, you must return the signed *permanent opt-out election form*, which will be provided after you initiate your online request.

When you call or visit the website, you'll be asked to provide certain personal information, including your home telephone number, name, social security number, and date of birth. The information you provide is confidential and will be used only to process your request to opt out.

While you may wish to stop receiving these kinds of offers in the mail, especially if you're not in the market for a new credit card or insurance policy, or want to stop mailbox clutter, remember that you'll also be missing out on many benefits of learning about what's available, comparing costs, and finding the best product for your needs. Because you are preselected to receive the offer, you can be turned down only under limited circumstances. The terms of prescreened offers also may be more favorable than those that are available to the general public. In fact, some credit card or insurance products may be available only through prescreened offers. Fortunately there are now plenty of consumer sites that compare credit card offers and insurance, listed in Chapter 9, "Practice Makes Habit."

If you do request to opt out, your request will be processed within five days, but it may take up to 60 days before you stop receiving prescreened offers. You can use the same toll-free telephone number or the website to opt back in.

And while we're at it, if you also want to remove your name and phone number from any telemarketing lists, sign yourself up for the federal government's National Do Not Call Registry. According to the FTC, it is a free, easy way to reduce the telemarketing calls you get at home.

To register your phone number or to get information about the registry, visit donotcall.gov, or call 1-888-382-1222 from the phone number you want to register. You will get fewer telemarketing calls within 31 days of registering your number. Telephone numbers on the registry will only be removed when they are disconnected and reassigned, or when you choose to remove a number from the registry.

FIVE

Checking and Correcting Your Credit Report

Now that you've ordered your credit report(s), it's time to check for inaccuracies, as well as make notes for areas of improvement. This process may resemble going through the sample credit report, and you can certainly use that as a guide, but this time, it's all about you.

When checking your credit report, you'll want to scrutinize each section. Log any and all inaccuracies and items up for dispute on a separate worksheet, spreadsheet, or notepad. You'll want to keep clean copies of each original report, should you have to go through the dispute process and reference any copies of these.

CHECKING YOUR CREDIT REPORT

Personal Information

Check to ensure that all personal identifying information is correct, such as your full name, address, social security number (when disclosed), and birth date. Note if there are any variations at the beginning and anywhere else in the report (particularly in the section reserved for address and name mismatches, toward the end).

Minor name or address mismatches are common, such as misspellings or omissions of parts of names such as middle names or hyphenated names. Incomplete or misspelled addresses, incorrect apartment numbers or postal codes are also common.

If you find any significant personal identifying information that is completely unrecognizable to you, make a note of the dates linked with these variations. This could indicate that someone else with similar information to yours has previously applied for credit, and/or these are just inaccuracies that need to be removed. In extreme cases, unrecognizable personal information combined with unrecognizable accounts means that someone may have used your identity or social security number to open new credit accounts.

Credit and Trade Lines

Scan your credit and trade lines very carefully. Look for the following:

- Accounts you don't recognize.
- Negative or delinquent information. This includes late payments, statuses (on time vs. delinquent, open vs. paid-in-full, etc.) collections, charge-offs, judgments, liens, and bankruptcies. If you've left any unsecured credit card debts unpaid for more than six months, then your accounts past the 180-day late mark may convert to charge-offs. This means that the creditor has charged off the debt from its books and decided it is unlikely to receive any sort of payment on the debt. Also be mindful of very recent versus very old derogatory information.
- Any cosigned or joint accounts. Confirm your status on these.
- Inaccurate balances. Check that your maximum charged or allowable balances on revolving accounts are correct. Note where they are inaccurate. Remember that most lenders or banks report 30 days in arrears, so if you've made any recent and significant payments to reduce balances this activity may have not yet posted.

Note: If your name is very similar to someone else's in your family, for example, your father is Bob Jones Sr. and you are Bob Jones Jr., in some cases your credit data may be mixed together. While technology and reporting has improved here in recent years, this is still a common occurrence, and any inaccuracies should be corrected.

Inquiries

When reviewing your credit report, ensure that you recognize the most recent credit inquiries.

Pay particular attention by looking for any hard pulls that you don't recognize because these are the types tied to applications for new credit.

Ensure that the inquiries showing are indeed yours. Also, look for any inquiries from over two years ago. These can usually be removed upon request.

If you don't recognize the companies by either names or addresses, then you have a right to dispute them and have them removed. An unauthorized inquiry without your express request or permission is a violation according to the FCRA.

Crosscheck Your Reports

Depending on which methods you used to obtain your report, you may have one tri-merge report that has consolidated all three CRAs' records, or you may have separate information across three single reports. In both cases, determine whether negative information is reported by only one CRA as opposed to the other two, and vice versa. Any discrepancies like these across the various CRAs should be flagged.

Now that you've parsed through your credit report, if you've found your credit report to be accurate in total, Congratulations! If not, then let's work to remove any negative or inaccurate information you found.

It is important to understand that in some cases you may be successful at removing negative information showing on your credit report *even if it is yours*. This process is detailed in the next section, which includes submitting a written dispute and resolution request with the possibility that the negative information can be removed.

THE DISPUTE PROCESS

A 2013 report by the Federal Trade Commission estimates that one out of every five people has an inaccurate credit report. On a national scale, that translates to as many as 42 million mistakes.

If you wish to remove negative items from your credit reports, you'll need to follow the dispute resolution request process. Requests are made in a formal written process, in which you will submit letters to the CRAs or creditors stating which negative items you wish to have removed from your credit reports.

From the time of the receipt of the letters, the CRAs have 30 days to take action. If you find erroneous information you'll follow the same process, either requesting a removal of the item (e.g., collection that is not yours) or a correction (e.g., request that a late payment be corrected to timely).

Use the template letters in this chapter for this process. You may have received dispute letter forms included with your credit reports. For example, here a sample dispute resolution letter from TransUnion can be found on its website and at tccbonline.com.

I've read that during the dispute process, you should provide as little information as possible regarding your personal and account information—you shouldn't even reference the credit report ID or enclose a copy of the CRA's credit report, because by doing so, you are only facilitating the reinvestigation process timeline. Forcing the CRAs to start from scratch with no information makes the 30 day clock tick faster in your favor, but it's up to you. I've been successful at removals using both methods.

Remember to stay organized during this process. You'll want to track your progress by keeping a worksheet of the trade lines being disputed, as well as the dates when letters are sent. Keep copies of everything, and never send in original copies of anything.

From the time requests are made, the CRAs are required to respond or remove negative and inaccurate information within 30 days.

Reinvestigation and Reverification

The formal terms to request that negative items be removed from credit files are reinvestigation and reverification though these may be misnomers. These are terms used only by the CRAs and those in the credit reporting industries. They are essentially the same as a standard investigation and verification, but since credit reporting agencies consider any compiling of a report to be an investigation, they therefore refer to the process of verifying that data as a reinvestigation. You'll see these terms referenced throughout the template letters.

Target Adverse and Negative Items

While the laws vary from state to state concerning statute of limitations on credit report items, for many states most adverse information regarding bankruptcies, collections, tax liens, judgments, some civil suits, and some child support debts are on file for at least seven years. Hard inquiries remain on credit records for two years. That said, many have been successful at removing negative information from showing up at all on their credit reports, *even if it was theirs.*

"Even when an item is accurate, dispute the information (if this is your course), since it costs almost nothing. There's always a chance that disputing entries can work," according to Dana Neal in Best Credit.[1] Sometimes, either due to faulty record keeping or noncontact by an original creditor or collection agency, the CRAs simply can't verify adverse items within the allowed 30-day time frame; therefore, by default they *must* remove them.

This dispute process is the starting point to removing negative information, and many will find that they can do so successfully, using the sample letters in this chapter, by having the CRAs remove the following items from their credit report:

Bankruptcies: If attempting to remove a bankruptcy before the end of the standard seven-year reporting period, you'll have a better shot after at least two years from discharge, and after you've disputed and removed any and all debts that have a status indicating they were included under bankruptcy on the credit report.

Collections: If the bureau cannot verify that the collection is legitimate within the reinvestigation time frame set forth by the FCRA (30 days), then the law requires that it be removed from your report. Collections are often reported by service bureaus, which are notorious for making mistakes, including transcribing SSNs incorrectly; if the CRA is able to provide verification documentation, ensure that it has recorded all information accurately, since any errors are cause for deletion.[2]

Judgments: Attempt to dispute these; otherwise you may have to arrange a settlement with the plaintiff. A paid judgment is far better on a credit record than an unpaid one.

Tax Liens: While you may be successful in having a tax lien removed from your credit report with a standard dispute process, if you actually paid the tax lien in full and it was under $25,000, then recent news indicates that the IRS may be agreeable in removing this item from your credit report. You may not fare so well if the tax lien is greater than this amount, and it is unpaid.

Inquiries: Hard inquiries ding your credit score. Dispute them to have them removed, especially if you don't recognize them. Remember that rate shopping, say if you're trying to get preapproved with a mortgage lender for a new home, within a 30-day timeframe won't ding your credit. Prescreened offers also won't ding your scores, as these are considered soft pulls.

Target Erroneous Items

In addition to disputing adverse items, you'll want to dispute negative items that aren't yours at all. When possible, you'll want to provide evidence, only if it will help to correct the item. Do not confuse this with disputing adverse information, which concerns the entire deletion of a negative item.

For example, if you have a credit card trade line showing a late payment that you want to dispute, you wouldn't want to have the entire trade line removed from your report, as this is counterintuitive; rather you'd just want the late payment corrected if you have proof of timely payment.

Dispute in Writing, Not Online

Earlier in Chapter 3, "The Credit Report," I mentioned that it's best to request your free annual credit reports in writing to be delivered by mail from each of the three CRAs. Not only does this give you a complete picture of what each bureau has on file for you, but it also prevents you from being subject to any limitations of liability and arbitration agreements that you must agree to when obtaining online reports.

When disputing negative information and requesting resolutions on credit reports, the same holds true. Online forms are notorious for forcing consumers to pigeonhole their disputes in irrelevant categories and for forcing consumers to sacrifice certain legal rights. Don't let the online convenience factor distract you from the recommended snail mail procedure. From a Fox Business Network article[3] in 2013:

> Sending in a dispute online may be quick. However, consumer lawyers say it's one of the biggest mistakes you can make.
>
> "The online dispute is all about the expediency of the credit bureau," says Cary Flitter, a consumer lawyer and law professor in Philadelphia. Most online dispute forms give you just enough room to state your dispute, he says, but don't give you enough room to back it up. "They want you to just say, 'not mine' or 'bill was paid,' and that doesn't always tell the whole story," says Flitter.
>
> Online disputes are also not set up to accept additional evidence, such as a copy of a check or of your Social Security card, say experts—and those pieces of evidence can be important later on if you do need to go to court to prove that a credit reporting agency isn't correcting a legitimate mistake.
>
> In addition, many online dispute forms contain arbitration clauses, which can undercut your consumer rights. "The credit bureaus bury waiver clauses in the click agreement," says Flitter. "By clicking, 'I accept,' you're giving up the right to sue them if they do something wrong."
>
> Type up, then mail your dispute instead. That way, you can include as much information and evidence as you need to explain your case. Also, if you do wind up in court, you'll be able to prove to the judge assigned to your case that you gave the credit bureaus enough information to properly investigate your dispute.

As mentioned above, send in your dispute letters by mail. Better, send them by certified mail, or with delivery confirmation, so you can ensure your documents were received. Keep copies of your dispute letter and all enclosures. Write the certified mail number on each letter so that you can easily match the certified letter confirmation with the original dispute.

The Magic Number: 30 Days

Credit reporting companies must reinvestigate the items in question within 30 days. During this period, the bureau will set out to ask the creditor if the disputed information is correct or false.

According to an article in the *Chicago Sun Times,*

This is not a human process, but is computerized. One computer is querying another. Essentially, credit bureaus are just warehouses reflecting information collected from creditors; they just report what creditors tell them.

"It's garbage in, garbage out," says credit expert John Ulzheimer. If the creditor agrees the information is wrong, the information will be corrected on all. You shouldn't need to repeat the procedure with the other bureaus. If a creditor says disputed information is accurate, the information remains on your report with the bureau. If a creditor doesn't respond within the required 30 days, the information is supposed to be removed.[4]

The last bit is particularly amusing, and the simple fact is that consumer dispute letters have high levels of success at removing negative information from credit reports because creditors are too busy to contact the CRAs to verify information before the end of the time frame allowed! If the CRAs can't verify derogatory information, by law they must remove it. Knowing this, you should know you have nothing to lose by requesting to have negative information removed from your credit report.

Minimize or Separate Your Disputes per Letter

If you have multiple items to dispute, don't try to dispute all of them together. Disputing single items or no more than two items at a time is the best practice, since for example, dispute letters that contain up to eight disputes at a single time may raise red flags and alert the CRA that you are in a ultra credit-cleanup mode, so don't draw attention to yourself.

Instead, use the applicable dispute template letter for no more than two errors at a time. For additional disputes, mail those in separately on separate dispute letters. The likelihood of getting anything fixed is better if the CRAs handle your disputes one at a time.

Make sure that if you are disputing a negative item that is showing only on a single CRA's report, for example, an account that is present on your

Equifax report and not your Experian report, you send in the dispute letter to the correct CRA. While the CRAs aren't obligated to notify each other, I've read that they at times communicate with each other regarding inaccurate information to be removed. Nevertheless, you wouldn't want to cause further confusion or draw attention form the other CRAs to any information that's not currently there.

Send Your Letters to CRAs and the Original Creditor

If you know which lender, collection agency, or other type of data furnisher (the ones giving out your information) is misreporting your credit history, send them the same information that you sent the credit bureau.

This procedure ensures that data furnishers have enough information to investigate your dispute. According to the consumer lawyer Cary Flitter in the FBN report, "That's another reason to do paper disputes because you're going to be caught in the middle." The credit bureaus process your dispute by assigning a category code to the dispute and sending a short summary to the furnisher to investigate the problem.

If creditors don't respond, according to the CFPB website,

> You can also log complaints with the Consumer Financial Protection Bureau. After we forward your complaint, the company has 15 days to respond to you and the CFPB. Companies are expected to close all but the most complicated complaints within 60 days.
>
> You'll be able to review the response and give us feedback. If we find that another agency would be better able to assist, we will forward your complaint and let you know.
>
> We also share complaint data with state and federal agencies who oversee financial products and services, and we publish a database of non-personal complaint information so the public knows what kinds of complaints we receive and how companies respond.

Follow the Formula

The most effective dispute letters are often the easiest to read. Don't try to incite legal arguments or use confusing, fake legalese, or other fancy phrases and words. Many letters that have been posted online as samples don't make sense, are ineffective, and will get you nowhere.

Instead, a brief, pointed dispute letter that states politely in plain English what the error is and what you want done about it is best. You need to be clear about what you're disputing and are entirely in your right to say, "The account was never mine," or "The payment was never late."

The letter must come directly from you, the consumer, to trigger credit bureau obligations for investigation. Luckily, the mystery's been taken out of writing these letters from scratch and template letters are provided for your use below.

Include Evidence, Only if It Helps

When sending in dispute requests, at times you'll want to include whatever evidence is available to support and back up your dispute. Of course, if you're disputing that the accounts or collections and negative information is yours at all, this paperwork will not be available.

When it helps your dispute, include documentation. For example, if you're disputing the reporting of a late payment, you'll want to include copies of monthly creditor account statements showing your payments posted in a timely manner from one month to the next without late fees. Another example of supporting documentation could be copies of excerpts from your checking account statements, showing the dates of outgoing bill payments, or if paid with check, a copy of the front and back images of the cashed check. If you dealt with anyone at the creditor concerning your issue, it always helps to include a statement typed out on a separate letter detailing any specific dates, times, and with whom you spoke at the company.

Another example would be if you're trying to correct a status of a collection to Paid in Full. It would be wise to include the respective template letter plus proof of payment of the collection with the cashed-check copy as well as any agency statement for reference. You're asking the CRA to contact the original creditor or collection agency for verification, so provide what document as proof is available. And keep copies of everything as the CRAs and other parties may have lost parts of files and documentation.

"Many court cases on this turn on the extent of the information that the credit bureau gives the furnisher. The credit bureau will say, 'customer claims paid,' but they will never attach a copy of the check," says Cary Flitter, the consumer lawyer from the FBN report. The credit bureaus rarely include the documents you mailed with your dispute (when they are reverifying), and so the furnisher only gets the bare minimum of information. It's up to you to have this information on the ready.

When you're ready to send in your dispute letter with supporting documents, again, make copies of your entire correspondence submission—that way you'll know exactly what was sent in and whether any information was lost when they ask for additional supporting documentation. Don't rely on the CRAs to keep track of every part of your dispute submission and stay organized with your files.

The Letters

The sample letters provided (Figures 5.1–5.5) are for you to repurpose as your own. They provide areas for you to list the item(s) you are disputing and also reference timing and your rights under the FCRA.

Demand Removal of Inaccurate Information, CRA (First Letter)
This letter is for credit reporting agencies. It is to be used the first time you request inaccurate or adverse information to be removed from your report.

[date]

RE: Reporting of Negative and/or Inaccurate Creditor Information

To Whom It May Concern:

I formally request that the following inaccurate and negative items be immediately reinvestigated. They are not indicative of my true credit history. In accordance with 15 USC section 1581i of the Fair Credit Reporting Act, I demand that these items be re-verified and deleted from my record:

Item No.	Creditor	Account Number	Comments
1	Sample Creditor	0000-0000-0000	Remove late payment information. Account has never been paid late.
2	Sample Creditor	0000000	Remove this account. Does not belong to me.

By reporting this information, my ability to obtain new credit is jeopardized. Please see the enclosed credit report for reference.

This is a formal notice, and I expect your compliance of my request, as well as a copy of the corrected report provided to me, within 30 days.

Sincerely,

Your Full Name
[Last four of SSN] [Credit Report Reference ID, Code or Number]
Your Address

Courtesy of The Credit Cleanup Book, 2014.

Figure 5.1   CRA Demand 1st Letter

Demand for Removal of Inaccurate Information (Second Letter)
This letter is for credit reporting agencies. It is to be used the second time, or thirty days after your first request for inaccurate or adverse information to be removed from your report.

[date]

RE: Reporting of Inaccurate Creditor Information

To Whom It May Concern:

On [first letter date], you received my letter disputing inaccurate and adverse items on my credit report. The original letter is enclosed.

Your negligence has caused me harm, since it has affected my ability to [specify the harm it has caused, such as "obtain new credit"].

Under the Fair Credit Reporting Act 15 USC 1681i(5)(A), you had 30 days from receipt of this letter to respond to my request for reverification of the erroneous items. Since I have not received a reply from you within these 30 days, the information was either inaccurate or could not be reverified, thus according to provisions 15 USC section 1681i(a), the items must be deleted immediately.

Please respond to prevent my pursuing my legal rights under 15 USC 1681n or 1781x, which require your compliance with the law.

Also, pursuant to 15 USC 16891i(d) of the Fair Credit Reporting Act, please send me notice of the removal of the inaccurate and adverse items, and a revised credit report to the address below. According to the provisions of 15 USC section 1681j, there should be no charge for notification of changes on my credit report.

Sincerely,

Your Full Name
[Last four of SSN] [Credit Report Reference ID, Code or Number]
Your Address

Courtesy of The Credit Cleanup Book, 2014.

Figure 5.2   CRA Demand 2nd Letter

Demand for Removal of Inaccurate Information (Subsequent Letter)

This letter is for credit reporting agencies. It is to be used for subsequent requests for inaccurate or adverse information to be removed from your report.

[date]

RE: Reporting of Inaccurate Creditor Information

To Whom It May Concern:

On [first letter date], you received my first certified letter disputing inaccurate and adverse items on my credit report. On [second letter date], another request was made for reinvestigation. The original letters are enclosed.

Under the Fair Credit Reporting Act 15 USC 1681i(5)(A), you had 30 days from receipt of the letter to respond to my request for reverification of the erroneous items.

Your negligence has caused me harm, since it has affected my ability to [specify the harm it has caused, such as "obtain new credit"].

Since you have not provided names of persons you contacted for reverification, per 15 USC 1681i6Biii, nor complied within the statutory period of 30 days, I assume that you have not been able to reverify the information I have disputed. Therefore, you must comply with the provision 15 USC section 1681i(a) of the Fair Credit Reporting act and remove the disputed items from my credit report immediately.

If I do not receive a revised credit report, free of charge, with the items removed at the address below, I will pursue my legal rights with an attorney under 15 USC section 1681n or 1681o "Civil liability for willful noncompliance." Your credit bureau may be liable for:

1) actual damaged I sustained by your failure to delete the items
2) punitive damages as the court may alloww
3) costs of the court action, plus attorney's fees

I have forwarded a copy of this letter to the Consumer Financial Protection Bureau.

Sincerely,

Your Full Name
[Last four of SSN] [Credit Report Reference ID, Code or Number]
Your Address

Courtesy of The Credit Cleanup Book, 2014.

Figure 5.3   CRA Demand Subsequent Letter

Demand for Creditor Removal of Inaccurate Information
This letter is for creditors only. Send it when demanding that they update or remove inaccurate and adverse information.

[date]

RE: [Reporting of Inaccurate Information, Your Full Account Number]

To Whom It May Concern:

Enclosed you'll find a copy of my credit report. The report contains the following false information: [state the false information, such as "30-day late payment in November 2014"].

I demand that you instruct the credit bureaus to remove this negative information immediately and notify me with a copy of this instruction.

By reporting this information, you are in violation of the Fair Credit Reporting Act. This is hurting me [state how it is hurting you, such as "by damaging my credit score thus resulting in my inability to obtain favorable credit"], and I expect your compliance within 30 days according to the Fair Credit Reporting Act.

Sincerely,

Your Full Name
[Last four of SSN]
Your Address

Courtesy of The Credit Cleanup Book, 2014.

Figure 5.4   Creditor Demand Letter

Demand For A Credit Bureau to Remove Inquiry
This letter is for CRAs when demanding that they remove an unauthorized inquiry from your report.

[date]

RE: Remove Unauthorized Inquiries

To Whom It May Concern:

I recently received a copy of my credit file and noticed that there are unauthorized inquiries on it.

[If you know that the inquiry was intended for review purposes only, and *not* for an application for new credit, state it here, e.g., "I have not made any applications for new credit on the inquiry date listed."]

This has hurt my chances of obtaining new credit. I demand that you remove the following inquiries immediately:

[List All:]
[name of creditor]
[date of inquiry]
[subscriber or reference code, if there is one]

Consider this a formal notice. I expect your compliance of my request by rules according to the Fair Credit Reporting Act, as well as a copy of the corrected report provided to me within 30 days.

Sincerely,

Your Full Name
Your Address
SSN

Courtesy of The Credit Cleanup Book, 2014.

Figure 5.5   CRA Inquiry Removal Letter

As already stated, don't go crazy adding too much information to the template verbiage itself—try to stick as closely as possible with what's shown in the samples.

Use the letter in Figure 5.1 on your first attempt at disputing inaccurate or adverse information on your credit report with the CRAs. There is reference to an enclosed CRA-generated credit report; however, you can choose whether or not to include a copy of the report.

Use the letter in Figure 5.2 on your second attempt, or 30 days after the first letter, if you haven't received any response from the CRAs regarding your first dispute.

Hopefully you won't have to use the third letter referenced in Figure 5.3. Use it if you don't hear anything from the CRAs after your second letter. It's highly unlikely that you won't hear something within 30 days; however, the letter is here for you just in case. It has stronger language and mentions the possibility that you will pursue legal action for noncompliance.

Use the letter in Figure 5.4 to contact creditors directly about removing inaccurate or adverse information they are reporting to the CRAs. You can submit this at the same time you submit your letter to the CRA.

Use the letter in Figure 5.5 to contact CRAs about removing a hard pull credit inquiry which you don't recognize, and which may negatively impact your credit score.

Once you've submitted your dispute letters, you should receive written notification of any CRA or creditor resolution within 30 days, if not sooner. Just about everyone, including myself, has seen successful results at having most negative, adverse, and inaccurate information removed or corrected, with the primary reason being because the CRAs have been unsuccessful at reverifying the information with the original creditors. Try it for yourself. You have nothing to lose (except the cost of a first-class stamp) and everything to gain, especially a higher credit score.

FRAUD ALERTS, CREDIT FREEZES, AND CONSUMER STATEMENTS

If you are certain you've been a victim of identity theft, then you can place a fraud alert on your own credit report to dissuade creditors from issuing any new credit.

The fraud alert itself, in most cases, won't prevent the issuance of new credit; rather, it will provide a red flag to hopefully alert the lender to reverify an applicant's identification. Identification should be verified with documents such as a driver's license, passport, social security card, or even a residential history, to prove that the person requesting the new credit is in fact, the right person. This was the protocol when I worked in the mortgage industry, as fraud alerts were quite common on credit reports. When this occurred, extra underwriting conditions were required prior to full loan approval, such as the above-mentioned verification of identification or residential history with documentation.

Remember that any fraud alerts will also show in in the front or general information and alerts section of a credit report.

Some states will allow for consumers to place credit freezes on their personal files, which prevents anyone from opening an account in your name. This could be helpful if you suspect anyone, or even an ex-spouse, is using your social security number, address, and other personal information required, to open a new account in your name. After all, lenders don't often question spouses applying for joint loans, if a spouse has a partner's full personal information and perhaps even a power of attorney?

A vengeful ex-spouse could file a bankruptcy in your name because many districts don't require identification when a bankruptcy is first filed. These types of bogus filings will get recorded as public records and are criminal; however, some vengeful people are capable of doing such a filing, and you'll have to seek a bankruptcy attorney to get the filing expunged.[5]

If you can't place a credit freeze on your report, then the fraud alert would be your best alternative bet.

Consumer statements, on the other hand, are generally not read, not scored by computers' credit-scoring systems, nor do they have any bearing on any other part of a report. As first mentioned in Chapter 3, "The Credit Report," these will not help your credit score in any way and don't particularly help to explain derogatory credit. The expression *Actions Speak Louder than Words* is applicable here in that your actions to successfully dispute negative information from your credit report will be much more effective than simply stating the situation and doing nothing.

SIX

Improving Your Credit Score

When it comes to credit scores, we've discovered how the combined factors within your credit reports all have a say. We've also discovered that certain factors outweigh others.

Credit scores are generated from complex mathematical formulas and algorithms that weigh and measure these factors against each other. And while we may not understand the minutiae behind the metrics, we can at least manage our behaviors to raise our credit scores outside of monitoring and keeping our credit reports error-free.

CREDIT IMPROVEMENT TIPS

In addition to these pointers, you can skip to Chapter 9, "Practice Makes Habit," to see my recommended latest and greatest apps and tools to help you with my tips that follow.

Pay Bills on Time

As mentioned in Chapter 4, "The Credit Score," the single-handed easiest and fastest way to boost your credit scores is to pay your bills on time. Timely bill payment has the most weight toward credit scoring, so do your best at staying on top of paying your bills on time.

Remember, late bill payments ding higher scores more than lower scores, so it's harder to build an excellent score back once it's hit with a late payment.

Also remember that late payments are logged on credit reports only *after* they are 30 days past due, so you can relax if you missed your payment by a couple of days. Don't get into this habit, however, because late payments on credit cards may translate into higher finance charges overall. Creditors always note in the fine print that once late payments are logged, your APRs may go up, so be very careful about paying your bills on time.

Challenge Late Fees

As eager as they are to hit you with late fees and higher finance charges, creditors can also be somewhat forgiving if you call in to request a late fee to be waived. Again, just like the ball is in your court to maintain an accurate credit record, the onus is on you to call in to dispute those late fees.

I've been successful at having late fees removed when I've requested this from creditors, and I'm sure the fact that I pay my bills timely helps with these requests. Explain that you missed your payment because you were on vacation, or that you simply forgot this one time (if you are a timely-paying customer, stress this point), and the creditor will likely waive your late fee.

Set Up Payment Alerts

Technology now assists in so many ways by reminding you of bill payments when due. Also, not receiving a monthly paper statement does not mean you can skip that payment. Your agreement with the creditor is that you will repay your debt or the minimum amount due by the due date, so try to get it in on time.

Set up e-mail or text payment reminders. Auto-schedule your bill payments. If you have a mobile app for your creditor, allow a Push notification on payment date. I've also noticed that when you link your bank accounts to a creditor's mobile app, payments will get posted on the same day, if not immediately. This is extremely convenient and takes the hassle out of the two- to five-day processing timeline that was previously encountered when submitting a traditional online bill payment through a bank. It also takes the worry factor out of wondering, "Will my payment get posted in time?"

Keep Your Older Accounts Open

If you've got older credit cards with high credit lines, keep those accounts open. The older, the better. The smaller the amount charged against the maximum allowed, the better. Remember that your length of overall credit history accounts for 15 percent of your credit score, so keeping your older accounts open is a good idea. This also helps your overall credit utilization rate, the second highest contributing factor to your credit score.

If you are desperate to decrease the amount of credit cards you have, only close out merchant cards, such as retail cards that were offered at the time you were buying something—if you know you're unlikely to use them again. Add to this any cards with small available credit lines that you're probably not going to use again—the older cards with the higher credit limits matter more. Just keep it simple with less cards to manage overall.

Forget Older Derogatory Accounts

The more recent a negative item, the more damage it is doing to your credit score. As negative items age, they have less of an impact on a credit score. Years ago, it was ill-advised to pay off older collections beyond three years old because payment would then log a more recent reporting date and bring the collection back from the dead, ultimately hurting your credit scores. While the CRAs will say that they have improved this conundrum by working with collection agencies, I simply wouldn't take the risk. Some have referred to this as the creditor "dusty pile"[1] or simply put, "Let sleeping dogs lie."

It is also a bad idea to pick up the phone and call on collection agencies regarding your old collections. Collection agencies, through a tactic called "re-aging" will sometimes bring a file back from the dead and restart the statute clock once any new activity has been received, including offers to settle. While this is illegal, don't initiate it—imagine how delighted the collection agency would be to dust off your file when it has already assumed it won't receive anything for the debt. Let me be clear—this isn't advice to not pay your debts; this is simply the truth when it comes to maintaining and improving your credit score.

Mind Your Balances

Pay your balances in full monthly, or keep them low. Remember that 15 percent of a credit score was due to the total credit utilized, or amount owed versus the amount of total available credit.

How much debt you carry month to month on your unsecured debt— debt on credit cards—has a significant impact on your credit score. If you can keep these balances as low as possible, preferably under 30 percent of your total credit, then your credit score will be healthier than if you were being close to maxed out. For example, if you have a $10,000 credit limit, it's ideal to not carry a balance of more than $3,000 from statement to statement.

I realize that for those who currently have high credit card debt, this may not be feasible for a while. You'll have to chip away at your debt slowly (refer to the strategies in the next section), paying over and above your monthly finance charges to get your balances down, and that's fine. As long as you're aware and working toward the 30 percent or less goal, then keep plugging away.

Carrying very small balances on your credit cards from month to month, as long as you pay the amount due by the due date won't hurt. I'm talking about carrying less than 5 percent of the total balance, not leaving your balances close to maxed out, if you can help it. Monthly credit usage stimulates reporting and history and also shows credit management.

Ideally, paying off the full amounts charged every month will save you the most money from high credit card finance charges anywhere in the range of the 14 to 20 percent mark, and you'll be helping out your credit score a great deal.

Pay Down Your Debt

The amount owed in proportion to your maximum allowed credit has the second highest impact on a credit score. Your goal here is to not shift debt around, but to actually make a dent in it. Managing your debt wisely will certainly help your credit score, which leads us into the next section. Read on.

If you have high credit card debt, sometimes help can come in the form of new credit cards that offer zero interest fees for transferred balances and zero interest on new purchases for a period of time. While I wouldn't normally recommend the shifting around of debt, taking advantage of credit offers with introductory zero percent APR periods (the longer the better) can provide an opportunity to transfer balances from high APR cards to these cards, where your payments will have a more significant impact on balance reduction.

Mix Up Your Credit

Manage your mix of unsecured (considered bad if you carry high balances) and secured debt (better because it's tied to assets). If you've got a couple of credit cards, an auto loan, and a student loan, then that's a pretty diverse mix. Utilize the cards by charging small balances and paying them in full monthly and continue paying timely on those installment loans.

Credit scoring favors good credit usage and behaviors, so you'll want to keep your accounts open and paid timely. Some people make the mistake of not using their credit cards at all; however, if you carry little to no credit card debt, resume small amounts of charging activity to boost your score. Just remember to pay all bills on time.

Limit New Credit Applications

Don't obtain new credit unless you absolutely must do so. Each new credit card application counts as a hard pull, which hurts your credit. It also results in brand new credit being logged, which re-ages your overall combined length of credit history.

Just say "No thanks," the next time you're out shopping and asked if you'd like to open a new credit account because "it will save you x percentage on your total purchases for that day." Once they've got you, they've *got* you. Ask yourself, "Do I really need to open this card?" If you'd intended to pay cash, then do so. Or use an existing credit card, and pay your purchases off timely. Think of it this way: you'll probably end up paying a lot more for those clothes than intended, either in credit card interest or by a lower credit score.

If You Have Little or No Credit History

Perhaps you are just starting out and have no credit to your name. Or, perhaps you have just always been of a cash mind-set, so you've never wanted credit cards.

If you're finding it difficult to get a credit reporting trail established, then the first step could be to obtain a secured credit card. You can do some research for these online. On Credit Karma by entering your search criteria and finding out your options, along with card reviews and typical APRs charged. As of this writing, I chose the "Establish or Build My Credit" bullet, checked the "Secured Credit Card" checkbox, and voila, six card options came up.

Secured credit cards can also be researched on Credit Sesame's site. You can search by credit health, for example, "Poor Credit," "No Credit," or "Excellent Credit," and by desired credit limit and monthly payment, and Credit Sesame will search its database of providers for you.

Monitor Credit Activity

Many companies these days offer some type of credit monitoring service that will alert you in case of any new credit activity. These services are a great first recourse to discovering any outside attempts at identity theft or fraud.

When you sign up for credit monitoring services, you'll be notified by phone, e-mail, text, push notification—whatever you prefer—when credit activity takes place. Hard inquiries for new credit applications generally raise the biggest flags, since these imply that new credit has been requested. If you didn't make the request, then you should investigate the origin of the inquiry and the creditor.

For credit monitoring, I've used Lifelock (lifelock.com) for years and haven't had any complaints. I pay a small monthly fee for them to alert me by e-mail or phone whenever a new credit application is detected. For the price I pay, they also automatically request my annual credit reports.

Credit Sesame's monitoring service offers an extensive geolocating social security activity tracker, which can alert you as to the area where your SSN has been used for credit applications. The three CRAs also offer monitoring, but I think that the third-party service providers do it comprehensively and with better data and technology.

Generally, credit can be obtained when a person is as young as 18 years old; however in recent identity theft cases, thieves targeted the valid social security numbers of toddlers and newborn babies in for credit card and loan applications.[2] All the more reason to be vigilant about how and to whom you disclose you and your family's social security numbers. Any sensitive paper documentation leaving your household should always be crosscut shredded and disposed of properly. For security tips, revisit Chapter 2, "Getting Prepared."

A WORD ON CHEXSYSTEMS

You may have never heard of ChexSystems, but it's essentially the reporting system used by banks and financial institutions to determine your banking reputation and history. Financial institutions lose billions of dollars every year because of check fraud and abuse, which is why 80 percent of U.S. banks and credit unions belong to the ChexSystems network.

If you've repeatedly bounced checks, written fraudulent checks, set up online/outgoing payments without sufficient funds and neglected or failed to pay on negative bank balances and even had your account closed as a result of your activities, then your data is likely on a ChexSystems report. If you've consistently abused your banking privileges in this way, then don't be surprised if you're declined the next time you attempt to open a new checking or savings account with a bank. There's a high probability the bank is unimpressed with your ChexSystems history.

Now, don't suddenly freak out because the ghosts of two bad checks are creeping out from under your floorboards. *Relax*, and remember that banks are looking for repeat offenders who make a practice out of writing bounced checks, overdrawing their accounts, or leaving accounts unpaid with negative balances, charges, and fees. More importantly, banks are on the lookout for major account and check fraud. Red flags include when inaccurate personal information is provided to open accounts and other activities signifying money laundering and fraud. For example, attempts at opening more than one account in less than a three-month period, hints at a concept called "Check Kiting,"[3] where people take advantage of the float time of available funds to create fraudulent balances. A person may write a check to himself from one account to another, knowing fully well that the check will bounce. But this person plays the float during the time between the deposit of the check and the bouncing of the check, similar to how he writes bad checks in hopes that they will clear by payday. If he just blatantly writes checks with no intention of paying the balances, this abuse is called Paper Hanging.

You should know that ChexSystems itself does not have the authority to approve or deny any bank account applications; it merely reports your history to financial institutions. So ChexSystems is only the messenger, and you can't shoot the messenger.

ChexSystems also offers a risk management solution to financial institutions called QualiFile. QualiFile uses more comprehensive information than just past bank account history to predict the likelihood that a consumer will be a good account manager into the future, and in this way, mimics FICO credit scoring models.

This includes data from consumer credit reports, plus third-party entities that provide consumer financial and nonfinancial data such as check printing history, retail scans of checks, credit report data, and payday loan histories. All of these data combine to create a ChexSystems Consumer Score that financial institutions may use to predict future banking behavior.[4]

Bank Account Alternatives

So what happens if you are denied a bank account? The reason may not be fraud-related. There are options to getting you back on track, and hope is not lost. "Roughly 15 percent of bank account applicants denied regular accounts are instead offered 'second chance' checking accounts or prepaid cards."[5]

Banks may require money management classes with these second chance accounts, and new account holders must not incur overdrafts or write any bounced checks during a probationary period. For example, as of this writing PNC Bank's Foundations checking program offers a 90-minute money management course which must be completed before the bank will offer a debit card, albeit with limited withdrawal privileges. If the account is managed well, then the customer can obtain a standard checking account.

If you're shopping around for prepaid card options, just beware of the fees involved. As of this writing, Chase's Liquid Prepaid Card, which comes with a $4.95 fee and allows customers to deposit checks at branches and ATMs for free, could be a cheaper alternative to some second chance checking accounts.[6]

If you're curious about your personal ChexSystems report, you can obtain one by going to consumerdebit.com or writing to:

Chex Systems Inc.
7805 Hudson Road, Suite 100
Woodbury, MN 55125

ChexSystems is considered a credit bureau and is monitored by the FCRA, so consumers are entitled to free annual reports. If you're curious as to what a ChexSystems report looks like, you can also find a sample consumer report from the site.

SEVEN

Managing Debt

As we discussed in in Chapter 4, "The Credit Score," your credit utilization rate, or the total amount of available debt used on your accounts (unsecured and secured) is the second biggest factor toward obtaining a healthy credit score.

Aside from your secured debt, which is paid down according to a schedule and doesn't increase in the amount owed, let's focus here on unsecured debt, which is the most expensive debt and also the debt that is easiest to get out of control.

If you're overwhelmed with debt, or have dug a large hole from which you're unsure how to start climbing out, my first advice is to *relax*. There is absolutely no reason to suffer from unnecessary anxiety or stress because of debt. Losing sleep and worrying night and day about circumstantial debt isn't going to help you get out of it, so accept the fact that you are in debt and begin thinking about how and when you can get out of it.

During two major periods of my adult life, I struggled with credit card debt: the first was during a transitional period when I moved to Atlanta after graduating from college, and the second was when I was trying to find steady employment after moving back to the U.S. from living and working overseas. I was on my own and just trying to keep my living expenses paid and myself fed and clothed, month-to-month, and absolutely refused to ask anyone, especially not family, for help. Instead, I emptied out my retirement funds and used credit cards to keep me going. In hindsight, this may not have been the wisest decision according to most wealth managers, however at that time it was my only source of liquidity, and that trumped every other logic in the book.

Ironically enough, it was due to my excellent credit score from prior years that had established high-credit spending limits on my cards, and these ultimately floated me (no, *saved* me) during that second transitional period in my life. I didn't max out my cards; in this case, credit was my savior, but it also drove me to work even harder so that I could eventually pay off the debt.

CREDIT CARD DEBT IS THE COSTLIEST DEBT

Credit card debt is the most suffocating debt of all, and the feeling of constantly digging and getting nowhere is a feeling to which I can relate all too well. Don't let it drive you crazy. With an action plan and being diligent to not overextend yourself, you can slowly get to a point where your credit card debt is neither bringing you, nor your credit score down.

While I'm not an expert in credit card debt counseling, I know that in my situation I was able to throw small chunks of my salary at this mountain of debt—some months in larger chunks, others in smaller chunks—until I had a small enough balance to wipe out. While this section aims to provide some very helpful tips on how to manage your debt, if you feel you are absolutely in over your head, or a major life event such as unemployment, or a medical issue or anything is preventing you from being able to pay down any of your debt, then skipping to the next section may be more appropriate for you.

DEBT MANAGEMENT TIPS

For those of you who are in the limbo phase of, "Should I pay-down debt," or "Should I file bankruptcy," understand that there are two types of personal bankruptcy: the first, known as Chapter 7 Bankruptcy, allows for most or all of your debts to be discharged or canceled. The second, known as Chapter 13 Bankruptcy, schedules your debt for repayment over a period of time. If you are considering either of the two options, then it is highly recommended that you seek out someone with expertise, such as a bankruptcy trustee or attorney. Sometimes all it takes is a professional's advice and helping hand to steer you in the right direction.

In my research for this book, I came across a professional debt management advisor who is Chris Welker, a bankruptcy trustee out of Ontario, Canada. Chris is the owner of Welker & Associates, a business he took over from his father, who was in the same line of work years ago. While his main role is to assist persons who are going through the bankruptcy process, he also serves as a debt counselor to assist those for whom bankruptcy is not the necessary option. I had the fortune to get in touch and ask pertinent questions regarding bankruptcy:

SC: What is your role as during the bankruptcy process?

CW: *The analogy I use is that of a referee. As a trustee in bankruptcy I am an officer of the court, licensed by the federal government. My job is to represent the interests of creditors and debtors and to make sure that the rules are being followed and enforced properly.*

SC: Is bankruptcy always considered a last resort, if your attempts to help clients with debt management do not work?

CW: *When I meet with clients we always review their financial situation and discuss the following options:*

1. *Can you dig yourself out of debt on your own? How deep is the hole and what have you got to dig with in terms of assets and income?*
2. *Could you/should you make a consumer proposal? How much, if anything can you afford to pay to your creditors?*
3. *Is bankruptcy your only/best option?*

Chris also maintains a large digital presence through his firm's blog, and on Quora, the Internet question-and-answer site where its community members answer just about every head-scratching question in the free world.

As of this writing, Chris' writings and advice were hands down the most comprehensive and helpful I'd found in the area of debt management, so he also graciously allowed me to share excerpts which answer some frequently asked questions regarding debt management:

Chris Welker's Tips for Getting out of Debt

If you are going to try to dig yourself out of debt without filing personal bankruptcy or settling on your debts for less than the total amount owed with your creditors, you need to have a plan (I discuss more on debt settlement in the next section; note that the DIY approach is certainly not for the faint of heart and damages your credit rating in the short term).

Chris' recommended approach for a debt reduction plan would be to gather your statements, find the fine print regarding your APR and finance charges being charged per debt, and position them in the order of highest rate charged. You would then want to allocate as much as possible toward the highest interest rate debts first. One of the biggest mistakes people make when they are trying to pay off their debts without any professional assistance is that they pay each creditor only bit by bit.

The problem with this approach is that your payments quickly get eaten up by interest charges. By paying off the highest-interest-rate creditors first, you maximize the effectiveness of your payment.

As with any plan, Chris says the key is to monitor its effectiveness. You must ensure that you are actually getting out of debt. The best way to monitor the effectiveness of your repayment plan is to take all of your bills each month and add up the total amount owed. You would need to do this on a monthly basis to check that your total debt across your balances and your finance charges are decreasing month by month.[1]

Should I Save or Pay Off Debt?

Rachelle asked: I am trying to save money up for an emergency fund but I have a heavy debt load. Is it better if I pay off my debt more aggressively or continue to save and pay my debt?

CW: *This is a common dilemma people have when deciding what to do with their money. The answer to your question depends on the interest rate you are paying on your debt and the expected rate of return you might be able to earn on your savings or investments.*

For example, if you could choose between the following two investments which would you choose?

Investment A: guaranteed rate of return of 19 percent
Investment B: nonguaranteed rate of return of 10 percent

In this scenario you would obviously choose Investment A. It has a higher rate of return, and the return is guaranteed. Assuming that an average credit card charges you a guaranteed interest rate of 19 percent, by paying off your credit card debt you are choosing Investment A.

When Chris explains this situation to people he uses the old saying "a penny saved is a penny earned." What he means by that is if you invest your money in paying off debt you are saving in high interest charges. These savings are the same as if you had earned interest at the same rate (leaving out tax considerations). Therefore, unless you can find a guaranteed investment that pays more than 19 percent he would definitely recommend paying off your credit card debt instead of trying to build up savings.

Given this advice, I then thought up a bunch of additional questions for Chris.

SC: What happens if a person takes your advice, and then has no emergency fund if he or she were to become unemployed? Then what? The person will have liquidated their funds on unsecured debt. Do you recommend building any sort of three to six months of savings reserves first?

CW: *Assuming they have paid down their unsecured debt they should have available credit to be used in the event of an emergency. While I would never recommend credit be used as an emergency fund, if there is no other source of money, what choice does the individual have? Regardless the option of paying down debt and saving 19 percent interest is still a better use of money than putting money into savings at a lower rate of return.*

Example: Assume someone owes $1,000 on the credit card that charges 19 percent interest and he just inherited $1,000. This person could choose to use the $1,000 to pay off a credit card or put that money into an emergency fund or savings.

Let's assume the savings account pays 5 percent interest. In this case if the individual paid off the credit card, he or she would be saving 19 percent interest instead of earning 5 percent interest. If the person pays off the credit card, $1,000 credit would be available that could be used in the event of an emergency. Plus, after the card is paid off, he or she could start saving and building an emergency fund.

> *I always tell people, "You can't build or rebuild if you're underwater (or in a hole). You've got to be on solid ground before you can start rebuilding."*
>
> *One of the biggest challenges I encounter when dealing with people who are struggling with debt is helping them to look at making a consumer proposal* (more on this in the next section) *or filing personal bankruptcy as a positive thing.*
>
> *A lot of people think that filing personal bankruptcy or making a consumer proposal makes them a failure and they can get really down on themselves. While it is natural and normal to feel some sense of guilt about not being able to repay your debts, you*

have to focus on the future. I tell them that we are fortunate that the laws of the land allow someone who is buried in debt to get a fresh start. I remind them about how struggling with debt has affected their relationships, health and jobs, and how, once they've dealt with their money problems they will have a better future.

One of the other reminders I have for my clients when they are in my office is that they are of sound body and mind, and that being in debt is neither a cancer nor a terminal illness. It may sound a little harsh, but people look at struggling with debt and having to file bankruptcy as the end of the world. However, the good news about money problems is they aren't life-threatening and with help can be fixed.

What's the Best Way to Deal with Huge Credit Card Debt?

There is no doubt that the interest on credit card debt can be a killer. Many credit cards have interest rates in excess of 20 percent. If you use Chris's Debt Repayment Calculator (at welker.ca) you can see how much it will cost to pay off your credit cards with interest over five years. One of the biggest mistakes that people make when they are trying to dig themselves out of debt on their own is making payments that just cover the interest charges but aren't really reducing the principal.

Chris says that if you are struggling to deal with *your* credit card debt and you want to pay back what you can afford, then the best option might be a consumer proposal for a settlement. By offering a consumer proposal you are able to stop interest charges, prevent creditor collection action, and settle your debt. While filing a consumer proposal temporarily damages your credit rating, it is often the best approach for people dealing with large credit card debt.

Don't make the mistake of focusing on your credit rating. While credit rating is important, improving your financial health is far more important. You can always rebuild your credit rating, but if you don't have a plan to get out of debt you will continue to struggle.

If You Need to Manage Your Credit Card APRs

In cases of medical or job hardships, or any other particular setbacks in life, creditors will sometimes allow a reduction or freeze on additional finance charges to your existing debt.

All it takes is calling to find out what they can do after telling them your situation—it may be dire enough to fit their reason codes or special programs. Creditors often reserve these for people who may be unable to make timely payments or the full amount of the typical monthly payments due, and the programs may last for set time periods of six months to a year or more. In exchange for enrolling in these programs, some creditors may also put a hold on your account preventing you from making additional purchases and adding to your existing debt. Of course, you won't know what options you have until you call, so if you're hesitant about picking up the phone, find the time to call each of your creditors and discuss these options which could bring some much needed relief.

Ask if you can make a lesser monthly payment. This would be your best bet if you are still able to manage a little bit of a monthly payment, barring any plans for a DIY debt settlement.

You'll be glad you called—anything to help reduce the amount of interest charged and APRs every month. The goal here is to understand what, if any, options you have, at managing or keeping your balances low. Double-check that by enrolling yourself in any reduced APR or APR-freezing programs, creditors will continue reporting to the CRAs that you are making timely payments. (Creditors can start reporting derogatory payments if a bill is 30 days overdue.)

Should I Pay Down My Mortgage Balance or Pay Off My Credit Card?

Investment A: guaranteed rate of return of 19 percent
Investment B: guaranteed rate of return of 5 percent

In this example, provided by Chris Welker, suppose that Investment A is your credit card debt and Investment B is your mortgage. Many credit cards charge interest of at least 19 percent. By paying down your credit card debt you are saving (earning) interest at a rate of 19 percent. Mortgage rates are typically under 5 percent. Therefore by paying down your mortgage you are saving (earning) interest at a rate of 5 percent.

Obviously in Chris' example you would choose Investment A because you would want to earn the highest guaranteed rate of return possible. When you're trying to dig yourself out of debt paying the creditor that is charging high(er) interest first will allow you to save (earn) the maximum amount of interest.

If you are struggling with credit card debt you want to make sure that you have a plan to become totally debt free. "Many people who try to dig themselves out of debt on their own fall into the trap of 'treading water.'

If you find that you're making payments but your total amount of debt is not reducing on a monthly basis, then he recommends reviewing your options. You may want to consider filing a consumer proposal.[2]

DEBT SOLUTIONS

What if you are beyond able to make any payments toward your debts? What if, the strategies above are just out of your reach? If you've run into a very difficult situation—such as job loss or medical hardship—that has left you struggling to pay even basic living costs, where paying toward your existing debts is all but impossible, there are also alternatives outlined in the following text.

While the consumer page at the Federal Trade Commission provides initial tips on managing debt, debt consolidation, bankruptcy, and debt settlement,[3] I've expanded on these very topics. Choosing the right path to managing your debt must be a well-informed one, and you won't know how or when to strike unless you know your options up front.

Settle, Consolidate, Manage, or Repair

In the past decade, companies who claim to help you manage debt, settle debt, consolidate debt, and clean up your credit have cropped up. But what do they actually *do* and are they legitimate? Like you, I've been confused by their promotions that have crossed over into mainstream media and ended up not knowing what's what. So rather than attempt to provide my definitions, I sought the help of the CEO and Founder of American Credit Repair (ACR), Steve White, to help break down this and my many other questions concerning consumer resources for debt management and credit repair:

SC: What are the different types of debt relief strategies and the companies that offer help? For example, there is a lot of noise about debt *settlement, negotiation, consolidation* and *credit repair* services. Are they pretty much all talking about the same service, and how does your company distinguish itself?

SW: *Although these strategies are designed to better your overall credit profile, they are not at all the same, and in fact, all are unique.*

Debt Settlement is not possible unless the client has fallen significantly behind on their payments for a particular creditor (or creditors). This approach involves offering the creditor a lump sum amount of money as a settlement offer in lieu of paying the full amount owed. Creditors can choose to accept this offer or deny it, and their decision is usually based on how delinquent the client has fallen behind. What's key here is that clients would need to have the settlement amount in cash available to settle the debt.

Debt Consolidation is when you take out a large loan against an asset and then use that loan to settle all your debt, resulting in one payment on your combined debt instead of however many original payments you may have been paying to all your creditors. With this plan you're essentially collateralizing unsecured debt against your home or other personal property.

Debt Management is when you deal directly with a credit counselor who contacts your creditors for you and works out a pre-determined payment schedule that can fit within your monthly budget. You make one payment every month to the credit counseling service, which then disperses your money to each creditor equally for the negotiated monthly amounts. This is an excellent way to still make your payments on time to your creditors and not have late payments show up on your report. Unfortunately this plan almost always leaves a mark on each account that is being managed by the debt management plan, which triggers a huge drop in the clients' credit scores until the program is completed.

Credit Repair involves verifying the accuracy with which any account has been reported to the credit bureaus and is best done through a professional agency, but can be done by the clients themselves through the dispute process (see Chapter 5, "Checking and Correcting Your Credit Report"). *Credit repair involves verifying how each account listed on a clients' credit report has been reported. When questioned, creditors must provide verification within 30 days to the credit bureaus proving the account in question has been reported in accordance with the Fair Credit Reporting Act. Any account that has not been reported to the credit bureaus according to this law or verified within 30 days must be deleted by the credit bureaus.*

Our firm specializes in credit repair services, and offers every client a very specific road map to follow to help re-establish their credit, combined with enlisting our help to verify and remove any inaccurate and unverifiable accounts. Any account on your credit report must be reported in accordance with the law and must be verified within 30 days or else removed by the credit bureaus.

SC: What is the average amount of negative items you've helped remove from your clients' credit reports? Is there an average number of credit score points you've typically helped raise per client?

SW: *Through the credit repair process mentioned, we raise a client's FICO scores anywhere between 70 to 100+ points on average within 90 to 120 days. The highest score increase we've ever achieved for any client in the past 11 years was 287 points for a single bureau. The largest number of negative items we removed for one client was 152 negative items; she enrolled three separate times and went from 176 negative items down to only 24 negative items.*

We have legally and permanently removed many accounts with balances upwards of $200,000. Accounts such as tax liens and judgments are a good example although we have removed credit card accounts and equity lines of credit with high balances too. It's important to note that we are not erasing the fact that the client still may owe the balance of the debt to the creditor, even if the account has been completely removed from their reports. We also remove foreclosures, short sales, bankruptcies and more.

SC: How many clients have you helped since the inception of American Credit Repair and what does the enrollment process look like?

SW: *We are focused on the extent to which we can help potential clients, not the number of clients who enroll with us. That said we have helped approximately 15,000 clients in the past 11 years since our company's inception. We are selective with whom we enroll and are not afraid to turn potential enrollees away if we feel we cannot help them. We conduct a thorough analysis of each potential client's credit report prior to enrolling them and present realistic expectations to each candidate.*

Unfortunately in our digital age it is also quite commonplace for dissatisfied clients to air their grievances in the blogosphere, on Twitter, or some other online variety. When I questioned Steve regarding two negative online reviews of his company's services, he stated that his company made efforts to resolve each of these matters with both clients—and with good outcomes. As we all know, online reviews can oftentimes be one-sided onslaughts toward businesses. Ask any business impacted by Yelp,

Google Review or TripAdvisor trolls, haters, competitors or just customers who can never be satisfied.

In the end, ACR reenrolled one client for additional work at no charge and ended up achieving satisfactory results for them. Steve said the client's promise to retract the negative remark, as of this writing, had not taken place.

The other client never replied to ACR's offer to conduct additional work free of charge. Steve considered the client's personal results to be excellent and perhaps even better had the client followed ACR's additional advice to strengthen his overall credit profile pushing his FICO scores even higher. According to Steve, "Unfortunately there aren't too many places for happy clients to go and leave positive reviews other than Yelp, where we have received many, many positive remarks from happy clients."

In closing, ACR's fees vary depending on the severity of each client's case and how many individual accounts must each be verified. The company guarantees its work 100 percent, offers a free consultation and free analysis of each potential client's credit report. As of this writing the cost to enroll was between $850 and $1495 for a six-month program, which can also be paid via a payment plan.

Settling Your Own Debts

While personal debt settlement was largely a completely unheard of practice as little as five years ago, a plethora of DIY debt settlers have now taken their stories of the process to online media and blogs. More news and research on the topic in general has also now put the process within reach for those who wish to take the creditors head-on. Many have chosen this route to be in total control of their settlement process rather than hiring a third-party debt negotiator to intervene.

You can settle your debts on your own; however you must be prepared and very strong-willed. You'll have to endure and stand up to creditors' and debt collectors' efforts and tactics at getting you to pay up, which can be downright aggressive and slick. And you're going to have to be very organized at managing and keeping track of the outcomes of each negotiated account. People are hired by companies to make debt collection their full-time effort and are rewarded accordingly, so don't forget they are professionals at attempting to get anything they can out of any debtor.

In researching this book, I came across the book, *Negotiate and Settle Your Debts: A Debt Settlement Strategy*, written by Mandy Akridge. In it,

Mandy instructs on how to settle debts on your own with consumer proposals, for as little as 20 cents on the dollar.

Within the book are actual template letters she used, as well as the creditor correspondence and eventual acceptance letters of her proposed settlements, complete with payment installments to satisfy the debt. All in writing.

Mandy became jobless, but tried to sustain her pre-job-loss lifestyle, so when her jobless status lasted longer than she ever expected, she ended up in big credit card debt. It happens to the best of us. I'm not advising that her strategies are a good fit for everyone; on the contrary they can be implemented by people who strictly follow the steps, are prepared for what to expect, and can ultimately deal with what could be a great deal of stress and damaged credit in the short term.

Debt settlement is certainly an alternative for anyone who simply cannot make payments or who has fallen so behind that the next step would be resorting to bankruptcy. An overview of personal debt settlement involves:

1. Stopping any payments on all unsecured debts that you are unable to pay. Immediately.

2. Waiting and avoiding creditors as they try to hunt you down to collect their outstanding payments. If they have your phone number, Mandy suggests getting an alternate cell phone reserved for family and friends. The goal is let the account go until it gets so far in arrears that they will be desperate to settle with you before charging off the account. "Their goal is to get you emotionally upset so you will write a bigger check sooner," according to a consumer who went through the process and was interviewed for a Fox Business article.[4]

3. Proposing a debt settlement for as little as 20 percent on the amount you owe. This may require some tough negotiation and standing your ground.

4. Confirming everything in writing from the creditor regarding any debt settlement and payback terms. Mandy advises to not fall for a reset of the process by sending in any money until you have, in your hand, the creditor's letter outlining the terms which are satisfactory to you.

5. Of course, that is the process in a nutshell, and much more detail can be found in her book and other online resources.

Again, personal debt settlement is not for everyone. Debt settlement will most certainly damage your credit, when creditors and collection agencies continue reporting delinquent payments on your accounts.

What I've come across is that if you absolutely cannot make your debt payments say, on your costliest debt, then this is a possible solution once you've stopped payments. If you decide to try to settle, you'll need to decide whether to do it yourself. According to a Fox Business article, with DIY debt settlement:[5]

You'll save money on any fees you'd be paying debt counseling or consolidation companies to negotiate on your behalf. Also, you may have an easier time with creditors, since your creditors and collectors will know they're dealing directly with you instead of a middleman, who may be tougher to work with. Creditors might go easier on you. "Collectors who know they're dealing with a debt settlement company might get more aggressive—and may even be more likely to sue. Why? Because they know they're competing with other creditors and that they might not see any money for a long time because many debt settlement companies put consumers on three- or four-year plans," Strauss says. But if you're on your own, "you're just a normal Joe Schmo account to the collector," said Jared Strauss, a former debt collector who now offers debt settlement services, in a Fox Business article.

Personal debt settlement requires a lot of time and energy. That said it might be too much for someone whose financial problems are due to loss or medical hardship, as they are already overburdened to take too much else on, and cannot deal with talking to creditors and collectors.

Finally, here's another excerpt from a Fox Business article on the subject, which I think sums the process up rather nicely:

Eight Steps to Settle Debts Like a Pro

Debt settlement experts and consumers who have been there say your approach can make a big difference in whether you succeed at settlement. Here are eight tips to increase your chances:

Get expert advice. Before you take the plunge, consult a tax accountant about the tax implications of settlement, experts say. The Internal Revenue Service counts debt written off in a settlement as income. The last thing you want to do is transfer your credit card problems to the IRS, says Strauss.

Plan your timeline. It's important to settle your debts quickly to increase your chance of success and cut your risk of being sued, Strauss says. "Twelve months or less is ideal, and I'd never go beyond 24 months," he says. It's essential to take a realistic look at your finances and assets to see how quickly you could come up with the money to make lump sum payments totaling 30 percent or 40 percent of your debts, he says. You should also figure that your balance will go up about 10 percent within the first six months of delinquency due to interest and penalties, Strauss says.

Know the typical collection cycle. With credit card debt, an account might charge off when it's 180 days past due, Strauss says. At that point, the account typically would be sent to the recovery department of the bank, and you could start negotiating a settlement, he says. After a month or two, it might be sent to a collection agency. After about six months, a collection agency might consider sending the debt to a collection attorney, Strauss says.

Find sources of money. Finding assets or other ways to come up with cash, aside from just saving, will increase your chances of success, Strauss says. "Do you have an extra car you're not using, or is that Harley-Davidson sitting in the garage 100 percent necessary?" Strauss says. Other assets to look at include collectibles such as baseball cards, coins and antiques. Or you could consider refinancing a mortgage, getting a loan from family or taking on a second job.

Take the emotion out. "Treat debt settlement like a business," says Kenny Golde, who created an Apple store app called "Do-It-Yourself Debt Settlement." Consumers tend to feel guilt, shame and fear about debt they can't manage, he says. "Banks will take advantage of that." For them, it's just a numbers game. They're in the business of lending money and a certain percentage of borrowers will default, Golde says.

Set up a system to manage calls. The average consumer settling debts has about six accounts, Strauss says. Multiply that by several calls a day—especially if the collection agency is like most and uses a predictive dialer (hardware or software that increases call answer rates). "It's crazy," he says. He recommends using technology to counterattack: Assign the collectors a silent ring tone on your cellphone to manage calls. Charles Phelan, founder of ZipDebt.com, recommends getting collections calls routed to another phone—a magicJack, a second cellphone or even Skype. Then, Phelan says, listen to the messages daily and return calls on your own schedule.

Explain your hardship. "You've got to have a hardship," says Sandee Ferman, author of How to Settle Debts Yourself. "A hardship is not, 'I'm not interested in paying for this big screen TV I just got.' It's you lost your job, lost your spouse, a tornado struck." It's a good idea to detail your situation so debt collectors can understand just how underwater you are, says Strauss, who has advice on how to talk to debt collectors on his site. The amount of evidence you need to provide will vary based on the type of debt you're trying to settle, experts say. For a credit card, you won't need to provide as much detail, but for a second mortgage, you might need to provide copies of bills and tax documents, Ferman says.

Get it in writing. Even if you reach an agreement with an original creditor or a collection agency over the phone, you should always get the agreement in black and white before you pay a penny, Phelan says. If you fail to do so, the payment you thought would take care of your entire debt could be counted as just a partial payment. "We're talking about debt collectors—They'll say anything to get you to pay," Phelan says.

Job Loss

If you've recently lost your job, know this: keep your head up and do not lose steam on a dedicated search toward your next work goals. Utilize all your potential contacts within your circle; spruce up your professional LinkedIn profile (as well monitoring the public components of your personal social media profiles). File for unemployment immediately; in most states you can now do so online, which takes the stigma out of going to the physical unemployment office. Don't feel embarrassed or ashamed for filing for unemployment: when you were working part of every paycheck went toward the employer's unemployment insurance. Now that you're unemployed, it is your right to file for your deserved unemployment benefits.

By the way, it wouldn't be hard to find anyone in your circle who hasn't been impacted by the remnants of the credit crisis. Ask friends and family for help or referrals for jobs; if you have friends who snub you, then frankly, it's time to find new friends.

I know what it is like to be on a constant job hunt and to struggle at finding and keeping stable employment. Many freelancers or self-employed individuals also confront the feast or famine that comes with contract work, but they have also found freedom by not being tethered to one organization. In the new economy, people are working on their terms. By farming out services for their skillsets on digital job sites sites like fiverr. com, elance.com, freelancer.com, odesk.com and others, they have found alternative income streams.

Bankruptcy

With a host of companies who can handle debt negotiation, credit repair, and even personal DIY debt settlement, you now have several options to getting a clean slate other than filing bankruptcy. While debt settlement damages your credit in the short term, you may at least be able to get many of those negative items eventually removed through the dispute process outlined in Chapter 4, "The Credit Score." Since bankruptcy involves the courts, any bankruptcy is a public record on file and will impact your credit scores for seven years.

Many bankruptcy trustees and attorneys also serve as debt counselors to try and assist clients in debt management prior to filing for bankruptcy. If the client chooses to proceed, as mentioned earlier they will have two primary personal bankruptcy options: first, where unsecured debts are dissolved, known as Chapter 7, and second, where a payment plan to repay creditors is established, known as Chapter 13. While Chapter 13 bankruptcy gives many a fresh start, it also often does not include the dissolution of student debts, and sometimes the courts will seize property assets such as homes, cars, or other items of significant value. But, you still get a fresh start; with either option you can rebuild your credit. Chris Welker says that "the biggest myths about bankruptcy are: 'I will lose everything, and I will never be able to get credit again.'"

Even assets that are not exempt are not automatically taken. A common example of a nonexempt asset is equity in a house. Let's say that someone has $5,000 of net equity in their home (after allowing for selling costs). Creditors don't want the home—all they want is the money, and they don't care how they get it. Obviously the property could be sold, but in most cases the debtor will make a payment arrangement with a trustee and can then keep their home.

In terms of getting credit after bankruptcy, it is possible. Credit rating is like a report card. When you go bankrupt or make a consumer proposal you get a bad mark on your report card. It is possible to get good marks in the future that will improve your average. The only way to rebuild credit is to borrow money and pay it back, but the difficulty for people who have recently gone through a bankruptcy or have bad credit is in securing a new loan or credit card. In this situation, there are two ways people with damaged credit are able to improve their credit enough to become loan-worthy again:

1. Secured credit card
2. Help from a cosigner

Obtaining a secured credit card is something you can do on your own without anyone else's assistance, and in the event that you are unable to manage your new credit card your debt does not become someone else's problem (refer to the first section of this chapter for resources on secured credit cards). As mentioned earlier, a secured credit card also established credit for those with little to no credit history.

YOUR RIGHTS

Earlier in this book, you were given a glimpse into what the Fair Credit Reporting Act does for Americans—namely, it monitors the three CRAs and provides a free annual credit report, among many other consumer protections. Now that we've addressed managing your debt and negative credit such as collections, you should also be aware of your rights under the Fair Debt Collection Practices Act.

The Fair Debt Collection Practices Act

The Federal Trade Commission enforces the FDCPA, which "prohibits debt collectors from using abusive, unfair, or deceptive practices to collect from you."[6]

The basic tenets of the FDCPA protect certain consumer rights, including preventing collectors from doing the following:

• Contacting you between the hours of 9 P.M. and 8 A.M.

• Contacting you at work if they've been told not to do so over the phone or in writing

• Harassing, oppressing, or abusing you with violence, public shaming, profanity, or repeatedly annoying you

• Providing false statements such as misrepresentation of documentation, suppressing their identity and the amount owed, and also accusing you of committing a crime. They're also not allowed to say that you will be arrested, have property seized or threaten legal action if this is not the case.

On the other hand, debt collectors are allowed to contact other people, for example, neighbors or relatives, but only to find out more of your contact information such as current address, phone number, and place of work. They are not allowed to discuss any of your private details or any information regarding your debt. They are usually prohibited from contacting third parties more than once. And if you're working with an attorney regarding a debt, collectors must contact you through your attorney.

"In a nutshell, bill collectors from collection agencies cannot harass you by calling late, calling your neighbors repeatedly or talking about your debts, calling your work, or at all! This means that you don't have to be a victim, and you can take action to see that the harassment stops or doesn't occur at all. A cease-communication letter is a way to get debt collectors to stop contacting you," says Dana Neal, author of Best Credit.[7]

Get Validation

If you have been contacted by a collection agency, you can ask for them to validate your debt. If you request this over the phone or in writing, every collector must send you a written validation notice telling you how much money you owe within five days after they first contact you. This should prove that they have been enlisted by the original creditor for collection activity. This notice also must include the name of the creditor to whom you owe the money, and how to proceed if you don't think you owe the money, according to the FTC.[8]

In some cases, unscrupulous collection agencies which may not yet be collecting debts on behalf of a creditor will scour credit reports for charge-offs, then send consumers threatening letters demanding payment on behalf of a creditor.

An unsuspecting consumer might take the bait, which then gives the collection agency a solid reason to solicit the creditor's business and collect the debt on its behalf. When communicating or sending payment to a collection agency, there's no guarantee that your money will ever go back to the original creditor. Be careful and always request the validation of the debt.

After you receive a debt validation letter, if you continue to be harassed by the collection agency, you can tell them to stop all communications with you.

Use the letter in Figure 7.1 to request collection agencies not to contact you. They will then be unable to contact you again unless they are notifying you of legal action that will be taken against you.

Cease Communications Letter, Collection Agency

[date]

Collection Agency
Address
City, ST 00000

RE: [Original Creditor, Your Full Account Number]

To Whom It May Concern [or Dear "Debt Collector Name" at Collection Agency]:

I demand that you cease communication immediately and refer the matter back to [Original Creditor]. I'm familiar with the Fair Debt Collection Practices Act, and you must comply with this demand.

Sincerely,

Your Full Name
Your Address

Courtesy of The Credit Cleanup Book, 2014.

Figure 7.1   Cease Communications, Collection Agency Letter

Should you choose to negotiate your collections with the agencies, ensure that all details of your calls—progress, names of the persons, and times— are written down. Be up front as to the severity of your situation and polite when negotiating, but firm. Collectors won't help people screaming or yelling at them. When sending in any sort of correspondence or payment, be sure to send it by certified mail and keep records of delivery dates.

You can also apply some of the same debt settlement tactics mentioned earlier in this chapter when negotiating with collectors. The older the collection, the more likely they're willing to settle for less than the full amount, to recoup anything on the debt. Any collections within the most recent year will have the most negative impact on a report, so start with resolving those first. Anything beyond two years should be left to the dusty pile.

After about three to six months of trying to collect, collectors begin to get discouraged, and such accounts go into a dusty pile—that is, of course, until they are sold off and someone wants to try again fresh, or a debtor actually calls and wants to talk about it (or worse, sends in money)!

Renewed interest could also cause fresh skip tracing and legal activity, so it's best to weigh your options carefully when you consider contacting collectors about old debts. Depending on the state of residence, some have date reset provisions where a debt collection statute can be reset with any payment, so don't open yourself up to be harassed. If you're unsure about an old collection belonging to you, it's best to go the dispute process with the CRA instead of contacting the collection agency or the original creditor.[9]

To read more about the FDCPA, go to the FTC's debt collection page at www.consumer.ftc.gov.

A WORD ON STUDENT LOANS

The cost of secondary education in the United States has skyrocketed, and it's no surprise that more families and students turn to financial assistance to bankroll tuition costs. Of the 20 million Americans attending college every year, close to 12 million—or 60 percent—borrow annually to help cover with tuition costs.[10]

As of this writing, there is roughly somewhere between $902 billion and $1 trillion in total outstanding student loan debt in the United States today. The Federal Reserve Bank of New York reports $902 billion,[11] whereas the Consumer Finance Protection Bureau reports $1 trillion.[12]

Going to college obviously has a price tag. If you're going the private college route, then you can expect to pay two to five times the amount of a state-funded public university. However, if you're going to have debt, then student loan debt is the best kind of debt to have.

Why? Because interest rates on student loans are usually low, at less than 7 percent, which is less than the national average of interest rates charged for auto loans, mortgages, and definitely less than the APRs on credit cards.

While growing debate has come in the form of acquiring a four-year education and being saddled with debt, versus forgoing a formal program and instead directly entering the workforce and learning skills, or starting a business, those who do choose to pursue higher education must either bankroll the costs themselves or rely on financial assistance from the school, government or private lenders, and also banks.

That leaves many with the burden of student loan debt well into their professional working years. Even President Barack Obama and First Lady Michelle Obama said in a 2012 speech that it took them roughly a decade to pay off approximately $120,000 in student loan debt, from their combined Ivy League college and graduate school educations. Judging from the last five years of our nation's tough job market, I'm thinking it will take most graduates today much longer than a decade to pay off student loan debt. And if you're interested in graduate, law, or medical school, that debt may be with you for a majority of your career.

According to the Federal Reserve Board of New York,

There are approximately 37 million student loan borrowers with outstanding student loans today. The outstanding student loan balance now stands at about $870 billion, surpassing the total credit card balance ($693 billion) and the total auto loan balance ($730 billion).

With college enrollments increasing and the costs of attendance rising, this balance is expected to continue its upward trend. Further, unlike other types of household debt such as credit cards and auto loans, the student loan market is incredibly complex. Numerous players and institutions hold stakes at each level of the market, including federal and state governments, colleges and universities, financial institutions, students and their families, and numerous servicers and guarantee facilitators.[13]

In October 2011, President Obama announced executive actions in the form of a "Pay As You Earn Proposal," which effectively capped monthly federal student loan repayment at 10 percent of discretionary income for college graduates, eased from the previous 15 percent.

This cap provided some relief especially to newer graduates worried about how they would pay back their debt in a tough economy. Student loan debts are shouldered by recent college graduates and other young workers who face lower incomes and higher rates of unemployment, than their older cohorts.

Around the same time, the Consumer Financial Protection Bureau also launched the Know Before You Owe project, which created a draft financial aid disclosure form to help students better understand the aid for which they qualified and to compare aid packages offered by different institutions. The CFPB is encouraging feedback from college students and families to improve the form and data in order to gain more comparative information about college costs and help make decisions about where to enroll. To sign up to provide feedback visit the CFPB's website at www.consumerfinance.gov.[14]

How difficult is it for borrowers to pay back their student loan debts? Of the 37 million borrowers who have outstanding student loan balances as of third-quarter 2011, 14.4 percent, or about 5.4 million borrowers, have at least one past due student loan account. Altogether, these past due balances sum to $85 billion, or roughly 10 percent of the total outstanding student loan balance. To put this in perspective, the same 10 percent rate applies on average to other types of household delinquent debt, including mortgages, credit cards, and auto loans. Does this mean that the prospects for student loan delinquencies are similar to those for the household debt in general, and thus no special attention is warranted? Not necessarily, since the figures are skewed due to deferred payment calculations, which suggests that delinquency rates for student loans are grossly understated.[15]

According to Equifax data, as many as 47 percent of student loan borrowers appear to be in deferral or forbearance periods and thus did not have to make payments as of third-quarter 2011. Specifically, 17.6 percent of borrowers had exactly the same balance in the third quarter as in the second quarter of this year, and 29.1 percent increased their overall student loan balance by taking on new originations or accruing interest to the balance.

Student Loan Options

A great, and probably the best feature of student loans, is their flexibility when it comes time to repayment. While in school, student loans are often deferred, which means they don't have to be paid back until after graduation. Tuition assistance today comes in the form of several options from the U.S. Department of Education's Direct Loan program (with the exception of Perkins Loans):

Stafford Loans

Unsubsidized: Available to all undergraduate and graduate students. Loan amounts for undergraduates are tiered depending on year of study, and for graduates they are capped at $138,500 in total. Borrowers do not need to make payments (principal or interest) on the loans while in school.

Subsidized: Subsidized Stafford loans are the same as unsubsidized Stafford Loans except that interest does not accrue while the borrower is in school, and the borrowing limit is lower. Both undergraduate and graduate students were historically eligible for subsidized Stafford loans, but legislation enacted in 2011 (the Budget Control Act) made graduate students ineligible for newly issued loans as of July 2012.

PLUS Loans

These loans cater to parents of undergraduate students, who may borrow an amount up to the cost of the student's attendance—which includes tuition, housing, and other expenses. PLUS loans are not subject to a specific dollar limit like Stafford loans. Unlike Stafford loans, parents must satisfy a limited credit check. Loans generally must be paid back over 10 years.

Grad PLUS Loan

Graduate students may borrow PLUS loans for themselves under the same terms that the loans are provided to parents of dependent undergraduates. Grad PLUS loans are meant for borrowers who exhaust eligibility for Stafford loans.

Perkins Loans

The Perkins Loan program is separate and distinct from Stafford loans. Loans are made to students from lower income families by a participating college or university. Schools have some discretion in determining which students receive a Perkins loan and the size of the loan offered.

Funding for Perkins loans differs from Stafford loans since funding is provided by the federal government directly to colleges and universities and must match one-third of the funding. The funding establishes a revolving loan fund, from which new loans are made as older loans are repaid.[16]

If you'd like to know more on the subject, a more in-depth resource can be found at the New American Foundation's site at www.febp.newamerican.net. A reminder that any suggested websites mentioned throughout this book are also listed at tccbonline.com.

Student Loans and Credit

If you're having difficulty paying back your student loans, what are your options? And how do they impact your credit score? If you're a recent college graduate, chances are that you may not have found a high enough paying job that will cover your monthly rent, living expenses, bills, *and* student loans. You then have the option to negotiate several options with the loan company who is managing or servicing your loan. These your options can be found online in one of three options:

1. Recalibrate the monthly payment and reamortize loan term.
2. Defer the loan, which postpones loan payments, with or without interest charges accruing.
3. Take a forbearance, which is a deferral with interest accruing.

If you can pay something monthly, then your student loan servicer may be able to recalibrate and lower your monthly requirements.

However, if you can't pay anything, then your primary options are deferral or forbearance, and *only* if your student loan is in a current status. If you let your loan go into default, you won't be granted either option. Therefore, keep your student loans paid timely until you've applied and/ or been granted either status. Sometimes your deferment or forbearance, once processed, will be effective immediately starting with your last payment.

Both options will allow you to postpone your monthly payments until a later date; with deferment your interest charges may be covered by the Federal Government, but in forbearance your payments are suspended and interest continues accruing. Both options will not damage your credit; however, your student loan status will show as in deferment or forbearance on your credit reports.

WHY DEFERMENT IS PREFERABLE TO FORBEARANCE

The difference comes down to interest. If you're granted a deferment, the government will cover your interest on any *subsidized* loans that would normally accrue during this period. This means that your balance owed at the beginning of the deferment (on subsidized loans only) will be the same once your deferment ends and you pick up payments again. If any of your loans are unsubsidized, interest will accrue the same as in forbearance.[17]

With forbearance, interest will accrue during the period you're not making payments, so your loan balance will rise during this period. The same goes for *unsubsidized* student loan balances. When you resume your monthly payments, your balance and your monthly payment will be higher.

When comparing the options, deferment on your federal student loans will always be the best choice. Depending on the type loan you have, any interest accrued may be paid by the government. Keep in mind that you still need to qualify for deferment, and there are several specific categories.

For example, if you are requesting a deferment and indicate financial hardship or unemployment as the reason, your lender or the loan servicer may request backup documentation in the form of pay stubs or a confirmation of receipt of unemployment benefits, respectively. From personal experience I have found some lenders to be pickier than others when it comes to ease of processing deferment requests, granting deferments, and what supporting documentation, if any, is required based on your requests. Repeated deferral requests may be denied, leaving forbearance your only option. Don't consider this a stain, since both options will protect your credit. Should you not qualify for deferment, forbearance is the next best step in postponing your payments.

EIGHT

Credit and Your Life

CREDIT AND YOUR HOME

The New American Dream

To many of us, the American Dream is the dream of home ownership. At least, our founding fathers thought so. Perhaps Thomas Jefferson said it best when he stated, "A right to property is founded in our natural wants."

The American Dream has also translated into the unlimited possibilities for anyone to "make it" in this country—and "it" translating into getting an education, working hard, establishing a career, or even starting a business. But for many, the Dream is still building a life and raising a family in a home that you can be proud to *call your own.*

After the credit crisis of 2008, many families have had to recalibrate their expectations of what it's going to take to achieve that Dream, and many are just focusing on making it day by day.

As of early 2014, the economy showed signs of creeping back. Household debt—which includes mortgage and auto loans—hit $11.52 trillion, the figure's highest since late 2007 just before the credit crisis hit. "Even after a devastating housing and mortgage crash that resulted in millions of foreclosed homes and trillions of dollars of home equity lost, the majority of Americans have not given up the idea that ownership is representative of their economic dream," said in a report by CNBC.[1]

Are we as a country better six years later? We are certainly making our way back and have the figures to prove it. Consumer confidence is higher, household spending has gone up, and financial markets have traded at record highs. But that doesn't mean banks are opening the floodgates. Quite the contrary: banks were slapped so hard as a result of the subprime movement that they are either slowly scaling down or taking baby steps at mortgage lending. Lenders are taking extra precautions to avoid any risk of a credit crisis repeat. Also, while it can be perceived that they are overcorrecting themselves as a result of what happened, it will be a long time before any standards are majorly loosened.

While some of you reading this chapter may not yet be ready to purchase a home, understand that regardless of your choice to rent or own, you want to have the highest credit score possible. Without a doubt, your credit score is one of, if not *the* factor with the most significant impact on the overall lease or home loan application.

If you're a homeowner, or you've been one, then you know the role your credit score played for your loan preapproval and during the loan process. The scrutiny over your credit during the mortgage process certainly hasn't dissipated—as a matter of fact it is more rigid and intense than six years ago. There is no more easy money policy that was widespread in early 2002 through 2007.

Housing Squeeze on the Horizon

Housing is one of the strongest indicators of a country's relative economic health. If people are buying homes, then they are likely working and able to pay a mortgage. Growth is facilitated by mortgage debt being repaid with interest back to banks, who can then relend this money with additional interest to others, and the cycle goes on.

Behind the scenes is an entirely bigger business of loan servicing among banks and lenders, known as the secondary mortgage market. In the secondary mortgage market, banks' mortgages are bought, packaged, and sold to investors as investment tools known as mortgage-backed securities. If investors aren't willing to take on risk with these types of investments, then lenders must remain conservative when it comes to the products that bring in the money for these securities. They'll only want to qualify those loan applicants with top credit scores, good down payments for home purchases, and lots of equity for refinances. When banks don't lend as much, people can't buy as much—which has consequences; growth is stalled, and industries are impacted.

As of this writing, tightened credit has already impacted housing and stalled economic recovery. Housing inventory was low just before the spring 2014 homebuying season, despite spring and summer traditionally the busiest seasons in real estate. With high demand for a low housing supply, the laws of economics took their natural course, driving home prices higher. If the trend of higher prices and tougher lending conditions continues, many first-time homebuyers will be squeezed out of homeownership, which pundits claim will only contribute to a wealth gap in America.

According to the National Association of Realtors® , home sales priced at $250,000 or less fell roughly 10 percent in January 2014 from a year earlier, though they rose by the same percentage for homes costing more during the same period. Accordingly to a Bloomberg report, a challenge to cracking the housing market for first-time homebuyers is that in much of the country home prices are rising faster than incomes. Strong housing markets are built from the bottom, and so this only contributes to the worrying trend.[2]

"A home is supposed to be our ultimate evidence that in America, hard work pays off, and responsibility is rewarded," President Barack Obama said in an August 2013 speech in Phoenix. He stopped short, however, of calling for a home ownership society, and in fact warned against a return to the past. "In the run-up to the crisis, banks and the government too often made everyone feel like they had to own a home, even if they weren't ready. That's a mistake we shouldn't repeat," he said.

Home ownership rose to a high of just over 69 percent during the housing boom after averaging around 65 percent for much of the previous decade, according to the U.S. Census. It has been falling steadily since, now down to 65.2 percent.[3]

As of this writing, the U.S. Senate Committee was considering a bill to axe Fannie Mae (FNMA) and Freddie Mac (FHLMC), the two government-backed mortgage enterprises created to facilitate housing and lending opportunities for Americans. Fannie Mae was created during Franklin Roosevelt's New Deal package in 1938 as an organization that would regulate lending guidelines, pricing, and most importantly, the secondary mortgage market mentioned earlier, the entity that purchases loans from lenders, freeing up liquidity to relend to new homebuyers, thereby perpetuating the housing cycle. Freddie Mac was created in 1970 to do the same.

"Prior to the housing boom, presidents from Ronald Reagan to Bill Clinton to George W. Bush touted the 'home ownership society.' They have been accused of pushing mortgage giants Fannie Mae and Freddie Mac as well as the FHA, the government mortgage insurer, to loosen their underwriting standards. The result of that push, critics say, was the over-leveraging of the American public,"[4] said a CNBC report.

In its remaining years at the helm, what the Obama administration does with Fannie Mae and Freddie Mac may shape the housing economy and accessibility to many earnest buyers. There have been rumors that private investors would take over if Fannie and Freddie were ever dissolved, and who knows what kinds of lending opportunities would be available if that happened.

The Sharing Economy

If first-time homebuyers are getting squeezed out of the market, and people are finding it difficult to qualify for mortgages, then the rental and sharing economy benefits. As can be evidenced by the company Airbnb. com and its many imitators, the home sharing and property rental site is disrupting the travel industry. The site allows travelers wanting a more organic (and many times cheaper) experience to rent someone's home or apartment, instead of booking at a hotel. The site has also evolved into a property management tool for landlords and owners, facilitating the renting of homes and apartments by tenants who are able to provide payment up-front, forgoing standard lease and credit requirements.

If you're concerned about your credit disqualifying you from obtaining apartment leases or even a home mortgage, then consider monthly rentals through Airbnb. A major drawback is that the properties featured on the site may not satisfy long-term needs, since many favor only a month-to-month or short-term basis.

A growing group of Americans are completely avoiding the home ownership route. They could be millennials (largely defined as those born between 1980 and 2000), many of whom watched their parents lose their homes, and who are choosing to rent for a variety of reasons—financial flexibility, job mobility facilitated by technology, and a preference for low-to-no property maintenance. Again, it will be interesting to see what happens concerning economic conditions and housing regulations over the next two years, which will certainly impact first timers' access to housing for the next or even two decades.

That Was Then: Subprime Mortgages

From 2000 to 2006, an odd thing happened in housing. Homes almost doubled in value. Basic economics teaches us that when there is demand for a limited supply, then prices go up. But supply was plenty, and prices *still* went up. Well, you say, maybe it was because people were richer and making more money. No. The average income went down from 2000 to 2004 as seen from U.S. tax returns during this time, which charted average incomes falling roughly 1.4 percent during this time period, adjusted for inflation. Housing values had steadily appreciated by approximately 1 percent every year since the Great Depression; however, within this time period housing values almost *doubled.*[5] A conundrum indeed.

So what happened? Subprime mortgages, that's what. The lenders who were offering loans outside of Fannie and Freddie's conventional mortgage guidelines started offering loans that were riskier in all aspects of traditional mortgage qualifications, particularly in income and assets requirements. People who couldn't normally have purchased homes were now able to scoop them up in droves. Also, with home values on the rise, home sellers and home builders were only too happy to sell at higher prices. Since home values are largely dictated by comparable sales in the area, the higher sales prices of surrounding homes impacted the overall, community, which impacted the overall area.

In 2003, I purchased my first house in Roswell, a suburb of Atlanta, because I thought that's what I was supposed to do as a young professional living in the south. By then, I had been working in the mortgage industry for only a few years. Most of my trade education came later on, from closing larger volumes of home purchase business.

At the time, I had only average credit and no money for a substantial down payment. Therefore, I closed my first home with 100 percent financing with a categorically "subprime" mortgage, a "2/28 ARM" or Adjustable Rate Mortgage, at 6 percent interest rate.

Let me break that down: while this mortgage enabled me to purchase a home with virtually no money down, the interest rate was only an introductory rate, at 6 percent for the first two years. After the initial two years, I ran the risk of my mortgage payments adjusting higher or lower for every year after, for the remaining *28 years* of the loan.

Beyond the initial two years, my payment adjustments would be capped by a margin, meaning they couldn't increase (or decrease) beyond a certain range with each adjustment, but what did I care about the fine print? I was getting an awesome house with virtually no money down. As a matter of fact, all I had to bring to the closing table was approximately $200, since the home sellers paid for my closing costs. Not bad for a young whippersnapper starting out!

In hindsight I probably could have secured a fantastic, fixed rate Federal Housing Administration (FHA) mortgage. FHA Mortgages are government-insured mortgages, and remain one of the most popular first-time housing financing options for buyers. They often require as little as

3 percent of the purchase price in down payment; however, the property must pass more stringent appraisal and inspection criteria. The underwriting process that comes along with FHA loans is also exacerbating at times concerning due diligence—only FHA-competent (and very patient) realtors and loan originators typically work with these loans.

My ARM could have turned out to be a very bad situation. In the end, I was one of the fortunate ones who managed to refinance once and sell my house before the bottom dropped out, despite my house lingering on the market for a little over a year in a buyers' market.

Subprime lenders were everywhere. Their loose guidelines were feeding the housing and refinance boom; investors continued to purchase the mortgage securities that were comprised of these loans, which only freed up more cash to further feed the boom. Low rates encouraged many homeowners to refinance. Many mortgages originated during that five-year period were risky, especially compared to today's standards. Especially the ones with very short-term adjustable rates—some adjusting monthly, some every six months—and with rates hovering right around 3 percent.[6]

Future clients came already sold on these mortgages due to ubiquitous marketing that promoted low monthly payments—never mind the fine print or risks involved. Fact is, there were many arrogant assumptions around this time: that housing would continue its robust appreciation, that borrowers would stay employed, that the job market wouldn't slow down, and that rates would stay low. As these domino pieces kept tumbling, many were left with few options but to try to keep the mortgage going until they couldn't anymore.

This Is Now: New Mortgage Rules, New (Safer) Subprime

Dodd-Frank

Components of the Dodd-Frank Act, which took effect in early 2014, were drafted to address the risks of ARMs. The two main components were to ensure that lenders began applying the qualified mortgage (QM) and ability-to-repay rules and stopping all loans with risky features like interest-only payments or negative amortization. Negative amortization occurs when the principal balance of your loan actually *increases* rather than decreases. Instead of building home equity with a conventional mortgage, these mortgages were losing equity.

Back in the day, negative amortization loans offered borrowers with monthly payment options. Two popular programs were Washington Mutual's Option ARM and Golden West's (later Wachovia's) Pick-A-Pay mortgage. These mortgages usually featured four payment options from low to high: minimum payment; interest-only payment; payment to amortize the loan in 30 years; and payment to amortize in 15 years. If you chose the second option, the interest-only payment, you'd never reduce your mortgage principal balance. If you chose the first option, the minimum payment, which was less than the interest-only payment, then the bank would *add* money back on to your mortgage's principal balance.

Obviously, the majority of borrowers got stuck or were tempted into choosing the first option, the minimum payment. And over time, this caused their mortgage balances to grow. I recall that these loans were being offered to homebuyers or refinancers at roughly 90 percent of the home's value. So when the rates adjusted and borrowers needed or wanted to refinance, perhaps to a less risky loan, guess what? They had added so much back onto their mortgage balance, and their house had lost value so they couldn't refinance and were stuck.

Over my career, I probably closed only one of these loan programs for a borrower and only because she insisted on having this loan product. I read elsewhere that if the complexities of mortgages could be analogized, then a basic 30-year fixed rate mortgage would represent simple arithmetic, whereas an option ARM would be calculus. The majority of loans that went bad during this time were ARM loans that permitted borrowing closely to a property's full value, known as a loan-to-value ratio. Compounding this problem were features like payment options and rates that adjusted under two or three years. Despite Countrywide being a notorious symbol for the credit crisis, there were many reduced documentation loans that didn't require income or asset documentation, as long as borrowers could provide a 20 percent down payment and had excellent credit scores around 760 and above. Recall that FICO predicts at 2 percent the chances of a person with a credit score over 750 making late bill payments.

Under Dodd-Frank, it's unlikely you'll see any mortgages like subprime ARMs again. In addition, QM rules cap the amount of fees lenders can charge consumers. The policy also requires lenders to ensure that a borrowers' total monthly debt obligations (including housing payments and all monthly bills) won't be too much to handle—this calculation is expected to be less than 43 percent of monthly gross income, also called the "debt-to-income" ratio.

Though many in the lending industry were concerned about Dodd-Frank's impact on the industry, the ensuing ripples were tamer than feared. Perhaps this was because 93 percent of home loans in 2013, the year prior to Dodd-Frank taking effect, already followed the new QM guidelines.[7] Also, the CFPB is clear to state that just because a mortgage does not qualify under QM rules does not mean that it is not an appropriate mortgage.

In June 2014, an article in the *New York Times* claimed that subprime is fading as a dirty word. To provide relief for first-timers and borrowers experiencing difficult to qualify under stringent traditional lending criteria, some bank alternatives backed by private investors are offering "sane subprime" financing. These loans lack the exotic features from predecessors of yesteryear yet fall under QM guidelines and yet allow for qualifying flexibility. Traditionally, any loan offered to a borrower with a credit score less than 640 was considered subprime. And with banks overcorrecting since 2008, purchase and refinance business dried up as a result of too many borrowers not qualifying for mortgages. Wells Fargo even lowered its credit score requirements for home loan from 640 to 600. How the new subprime mortgages fare depends on timing, response, market and borrower behaviors.[8]

Government Insured, or FHA Loans

As mentioned earlier, FHA loans remain one of the most popular paths to home ownership for borrowers who may not have substantial down payments. The credit guidelines for FHA loans can also be more lenient than traditional underwriting standards and in some cases will allow borrowers with scores up to the 600s, provided other income and asset criteria are met. It is advised to seek out a loan originator experienced with this type of home financing, as guidelines are updated frequently and outside of automated or computer-generated loan approvals, many FHA approvals are still determined by manual underwriting.

Back from the Trenches: James Dorcely

Since I am several years removed from the industry, I consulted a dear friend and colleague of mine, James Dorcely, the most consummate loan originator I know.

James has worked for over a decade as a loan originator serving the New York real estate market. As of this writing, he was primarily lending to the New York Metropolitan markets as a vice president and area manager for EverBank. He is known as the guy who gets it done, and his knowledge of New York's tricky condominium and co-op approval process and jumbo (high loan size) mortgages is unparalleled.

Over the course of James' career he has originated close to $1 billion (yes, that's $1 *billion*) in loan volume, which covers roughly 1,400 properties. I met James in Charlotte, North Carolina when we were both training with Wachovia Mortgage, after which time I saw him rise to the top of the company's monthly loan production charts. A reason he's found success in the industry may be due to his emphatic customer-centric approach to his business.

With James' extensive loan history, it was only natural that I sat down with him to break down the differences in the lending climate today versus six years ago. I asked him to give me an idea of what 2013 looked like for him, compared to 2009. According to James:

The most compelling difference between the mortgage business in 2009 versus 2013 is where the value of real estate is trading, and the amount of real estate inventory that is available.

In 2009, there were simply more properties in the market available for sale. The mortgage business was correcting itself, and a lot of mortgage products were becoming discontinued, almost daily. It was very difficult to qualify borrowers, when compared with years prior. Banks were over-correcting, swinging the pendulum too far to one side, and as a result, tighter, stricter and inconsistent mortgage guidelines forced a lot of us in the business to get back to the drawing board.

Between January and May of 2013, however, the mortgage industry experienced one of highest production levels recorded in history. After May, when the Federal Reserve hinted that it might start tapering the bond buy-back program—which had been providing liquidity to the Mortgage Backed Securities and Bond market and in turn kept interest rates low—mortgage rates took a violent swing upward.

By November, reports showed major lenders' application volumes at 11-year lows. In some instances, lenders reported up to 75 percent less mortgage applications compared to the same month one year earlier in 2012.

SC: Will the mortgage landscape change after lenders apply the ability-to-repay rules from the Dodd-Frank Act?

JD: *The landscape isn't going to be significantly affected at all. The practice of evaluating a borrower's "ability to repay" has already been in play in the mortgage business for some time now. Mortgage loans being financed through Fannie (Mae), Freddie*

(Mac) *and FHA for the next few years will not experience major changes. Very similar rules, like being capped at 43 percent on the debt-to-income ratio, were already built into the underwriting systems and engines for the aforementioned types of loans.*

Most affected will be your high loan amount, or "Jumbo" loan borrowers who based their abilities to qualify for certain mortgages on their banking relationship or level of deposit or other compensating factors. You will also find that interest-only loans are no longer available, which were very popular for my clients including Wall Street executives or other private sector executives, who had the bulk of their income deriving from an annual bonus from which they would apply a chunk to interest-only loans for significant principal reduction.

SC: Speaking of jumbo loans, what are today's loan thresholds, and why would a person choose a jumbo mortgage over a conventional, or conforming mortgage, since typically conforming mortgages have lower rates? Also, what are the current conforming and nonconforming loan limits?

JD: (As of this writing) In metropolitan "high cost" markets like Manhattan, Fannie Mae's loan limit is $625,500.

There are two major reasons that borrowers would consider Jumbo mortgages over conforming ones: First, rates. In the recent market, Jumbo mortgage rates have been more competitive than the "conforming" Fannie Mae rates which are for loan amounts up to $417,001 and higher. Second, Fannie Mae loans typically have lower savings reserve requirements. Of course, if a borrower's qualifications don't fit a certain profile and are an exception to the rules, then he or she could resort to Jumbo financing, because a Jumbo lender would have the ability to allow for out-of-the-box guidelines.

SC: What are the optimal mortgage qualification guidelines these days?

JD: *Typically, lenders look for a 43 percent debt-to-income ratio, 12 to 24 months of the future monthly mortgage payment and other debts in savings reserves, 2 years of job stability documented via tax returns, a large down payment, like 20 percent of the purchase price, or if refinancing, then a substantial amount of home equity, and for first-time homebuyers, proof of at least 12 months of timely rent payments. Depending on the strength of your credit score, you may be required to provide more or less documentation.*

SC: Do you see any sort of subprime or reduced documentation loans returning?

JD: *None at all. Especially since institutions would now have to put up 5 percent of the loans' balance in reserves. I see specialized banks doing some sort of "assets as income" bank loan by amortizing the borrowers' assets over 180 to 360 months, to create some sort of qualifying income, but a scenario like that would be only for borrowers with significant assets, very high credit and a very low loan-to-value ratio. In addition to the loan amount being borrowed, the credit score is obviously one of, if not the most important part of a loan application to a lender, because it's one of the best indicators of how the borrower will repay their loan.*

CREDIT AND ENTREPRENEURS

Credit and Business Loans

If you're a small business owner and you've traditionally sought out bank financing, or you're interested in securing some small business or start-up financing, then this section on business lending is just for you.

Small business financing has also morphed since the credit crisis. I spoke with a prominent private wealth manager and vice president for a S&P 100 regional bank based in Atlanta with approximately $120 billion in assets, and we discussed what bank lending criteria looks like now for small businesses:

SC: What are the traditional criteria and requirements for small business lending?

Answer: *Traditionally, we look for 3 years of tax returns on all Guarantors, a complete financial statement, Articles of Incorporation and tax IDs, valid identification, no existing record of a poorly managed account (i.e., a record on ChexSystems), solid credit scores of any borrowers involved (usually anyone with more than a 25 percent business ownership is required to be on the loan or line of credit). The big focus nowadays is also on liquidity. The more access to liquidity the better. Depending on the company and how fast it can get going also contributes to how much additional information we need.*

SC: Tell me a little bit about business credit scoring. Is it comparable to how an individual's credit is scored? Is it common for an individual to attempt to obtain financing based on his personal credit, if he has a fairly new business and/or he doesn't have any business credit history established?

Answer: *The inherent challenge with Small Business Lending is the lack of history. As the company is so new, the opportunity most often comes down to the underlying Guarantors of the company. The stronger the Guarantors, the better the chances are of obtaining financing. The most common small business loans take into account the Guarantor's personal ability to pay back the loan, and look at the history that individual has had using credit, commonly known as the "5 C's" of credit (collateral, character, credit, capacity and conditions). As most small businesses have no credit, it almost entirely comes down to the individual(s) wanting to get a business going.*

SC: In Metro Atlanta, what is your average small business or private banking loan size? What is the average in terms of revenues and/or number of employees?

Answer: *"Small Business" in Atlanta and most markets is a very generic term for companies under $10 million or so in annual revenue. Revenue is the most critical element banks will look at in determining the best place to help the client internally. It is hard to say what the average size loan is because there are so many types of needs out there for credit. As a result of so many changes in our industry, most banks have centralized their credit teams to stay on top of their lending books. This also is an effective way for banks to stay ahead of the many regulatory changes that have come about in recent years.*

Small Business is very different from Private Banking. Private Banking is more for Personal Banking versus Business Banking. Most banks are now divided into silos, and navigating those silos from the very beginning is critical. Unfortunately, a potential customer can spend a lot of time trying to get in front of the correct banking representative. When I started in banking in the mid-90s, I was trained in various areas of the bank including Small Business. Most bankers now are "experts" in their given silo, so if you're not in front of the correct person, you could waste a lot of time with the wrong person who doesn't have the expertise you need.

Along with Private Banking, you will also find Small Business Bankers (banking companies with under $1–2 million in annual revenue), Business Bankers (usually looking for companies with 2+ years of history and north of $2 million in annual revenue), Commercial Bankers (targeting larger companies with more than $25 million in annual revenue), and Corporate Bankers (targeting the largest of all companies).

More recently, many banks have brought in "SBA" Bankers that are experts in Small Business Lending. A great place to start when considering funding for your small business is by having a conversation with an SBA Banker, as they usually have a deeper knowledge of all of the various Government lending programs available.

SC: Since the economic recovery from postrecessionary 2009, has there been an increase or decrease in loan applications?

Answer: *I would say that there was a big drop in loan applications when the recession hit. Most clients wanted to wait or delay their decisions as the economic uncertainty made people play "defense" and not want to take on any new risks. It really does feel like the worst is behind us, but there still are many new factors affecting decisions. The impact of the Affordable Health Care Act, the impact of the housing recovery, the effects of Quantitative Easing, the international market uncertainty and all of the new regulations are still fogging the economic windshield. As people are willing to take on more risk, we should see more Small Business activity grow.*

SC: Would you say your bank's small business lending requirements are fairly competitive across the board with those of credit unions and other banks?

Answer: *Yes, we are very much in line with other institutions. Our SBA department has grown and is doing a fantastic job. Many bankers have gained tremendous experience going through the recession. When times are good, everyone seems to be an expert on risk. When times are bad, there are corrections made to mitigate and evaluate risk better. Most banks that have survived this mess are stronger and smarter than ever.*

The relationship with the banker is the most critical element in my opinion—a good starting point comes down to finding the best people you can. My best advice is encouraging potential small business owners to do their due diligence before going into a bank. Talk to other business owners, talk to industry experts and take ownership of decisions early on in the process.

Startup Funding and Alternatives to Business Lending

Before you build your business, before you get a project off the ground, and before your tech startup secures venture capital and the billion-dollar acquisition, your brilliant enterprise may be in need of some funding. As mentioned earlier, there is no way that banks would lend money to some pimply faced teenager with no personal or business credit history, and credit cards may not be a great (and certainly not the cheapest) option.

So if you're not interested in going the traditional bank lending route as described earlier, and you can't bootstrap, then don't fret because these days entrepreneurs are bypassing banks and getting some serious startup capital through seed funding, crowdfunding, and microlending.

These entities help entrepreneurs get the cash they need to build their businesses by skipping all the red tape and bureaucracy commonly associated with small business loans.

Crowdfunding

Kickstarter (kickstarter.com)—the granddaddy of all crowdfunding sites, Kickstarter mostly funds creative projects. If you're passionate about seeing a project through to fruition but need to raise some funds, post your pitch (usually consisting of a compelling slideshow and/or video) and watch your supporters and funds grow. Magazines, retail products, major films, books, inventions, and so much more have been funded on Kickstarter.

Incubators

For tech start-ups, incubator programs nurture promising companies with small investments, sometimes also taking small equity stakes. They connect founders with mentors and investors and provide a platform to show off their companies. Competition is fierce, and you better have a solid idea and development team to get their attention. The better the pitch and prospects for users, revenues, and scalability (even better if they are capable of disrupting an existing high revenue industry) the better the chances of acceptance. Examples of incubators are:

500 Startups (500.co): As an accelerator and seed funder, 500 Startups has nurtured some of the world's most innovative companies today. Some personal favorites of mine include the task person site TaskRabbit (task-rabbit.com). Seriously, I've never shopped at Ikea nor assembled Ikea furniture since finding TaskRabbit. Also, be on the lookout for Mayvenn (mayvenn.com), cofounded by my friend and business school colleague Diishan Imira. The company is disrupting the billion-dollar African American hair industry and equips stylists with extra revenue streams by selling hair product to their clients directly from their own Mayvenn websites rather than sending them to buy hair at beauty supply stores.

Y Combinator (ycombinator.com): Another accelerator, Y Combinator started in March 2005. The company also provides seed money, advice, and connections in exchange for roughly 6 percent of the company's equity. Some of the more prominent Y Combinator startups include the social news sharing site Reddit, Airbnb, and Dropbox, also mentioned in Chapter 2, "Getting Prepared."

TechStars (techstars.com): Finally, there's TechStars, which does essentially the same thing as the two other incubators mentioned earlier, whose most notable company was SendGrid (sendgrid.com) the e-mail automation company.

MicroLending

Pioneered by the Bangladeshi Nobel Peace Prize winner Muhammed Yunus, microlending, also termed microfinancing, has sprung up in recent years due to postrecession business credit tightening. It seems that small business owners with brick-and-mortar setups benefit most. Microloans finance much smaller amounts than those issued with traditional bank lending, and supply fulfill small business needs with reasonable interest rates around six to 10 percent. They also often look beyond a low credit score and continue to allow the small business sector to thrive—the only sector that grew during the recession.

Accion (accioneast.org): Accion is the nation's largest not-for-profit lender and focuses on helping women, minorities, and immigrants. With loan sizes of under $10,000 up to $50,000, the company has arranged nearly 13,000 loans totaling more than $94.5 million in the New York region alone, in the 21 years it has been in business. According to CEO Gina Harman, "These loans, on average, create two and a half jobs, which is consistent with the fact that the small business sector has been the only sector to contribute net increases in the last 10 years," she said. "So when a small business is supported, the business generates revenue, it becomes part of the tax base and it adds to the stability in communities and employment, which makes a $7,000 loan a pretty efficient tool for driving the economy."[9]

Opportunity Fund (opportunityfund.org): This company also provides "working capital to working people," as stated on its website. The organization is making several times as many loans as it did five years ago, lending between $1 million and $2 million a month and over 1,000 loans a year.[10]

CREDIT AND SERVICES

Ever wonder why, when you've just moved and are trying to set up your utilities in your new place, or when you've applied for a new cell phone plan, certain companies request to check your credit report? Why are they allowed to even do this? Can you still be a customer if you don't allow these companies to pull your credit report?

When you've just relocated to a new home or apartment, you'll have to go through the process of setting up your basic utilities and services. And most of today's service providers—electricity, cable, gas, water, telephone, and cellphone providers—will ask to check your credit report.

Service providers pull a soft report when checking your credit. Which means that they don't hurt credit scores, nor are they logged on a credit report since they're not new applications for credit. That said, what service companies are looking for when they pull your credit report is generally an idea of your payment history, residential history, and length of existing credit.

Those with significant credit issues could be required to put down a security deposit to start services, add a cosigner, or pay higher rates for their utilities. Even better incentive to keep an eye on your credit history and manage your score accordingly!

CREDIT AND EMPLOYMENT

If you're looking for work, and it's been awhile since you were last in the job market, you need to know that most companies these days will pull your credit history as part of the recruiting process. Credit inquiries are becoming standard procedures, in addition to work history verifications and criminal background checks.

Keep in mind that a company's human resources department is not usually the one obtaining this data. Rather, the company will contract with an independent third-party vendor who is entitled to complete these checks, so both the company and the employment screening company must follow the FCRA's guidelines on employment checks. For smaller companies who may be performing the checks on their own, it may be in your best interest to clarify what will be scrutinized during the screening process.

So the question begs: How much do prospective employers consider credit history when considering job applicants?

The answer largely deals with the type or level of role the applicant is seeking and the industry in which the candidate is applying.

For example, for those wanting to work in the financial and insurance industries, companies will be much more interested in an applicant's criminal background check. Obviously the company would want to be aware of any matters of fraud, outstanding legal entanglements, bankruptcies, and foreclosures (the latter two which are public records anyway).

Companies may also put weight on the fact that an applicant's solid credit record and prudent payment history are behavioral indicators not only of responsible financial management but also of future job performance; never mind his ability to do said job well.

Recently I spoke with Michael Karp, the CEO and Cofounder of Options Group, the premier executive search, market intelligence, and consulting company. Options Group places high-level finance people with top financial institutions and banks. I picked his brain on how a credit inquiry would impact even very high-level executive candidates' files, for the top and very public Managing Director, CFO, and CEO roles, and this is what he shared:

SC: Why do and what are employers typically looking for when they pull a job candidate's credit information?

MK: *In finance, it's crucial to know whether someone has mismanaged his own finances, because it could be a reflection of how well he will manage other people's, or a large institution's money.*

        The SEC was more successful in cracking down on Ponzi Schemes—where investors are paid out with other investors' money—after the Bernie Madoff scandal,[11] and all that publicity made more investors wary of investment managers, in general. To allay investor concerns, hedge funds have now also implemented a more stringent pre-screening process.

SC: For a top, financial executive role, what additional information aside from credit history might a prospective employer want?

MK: *For portfolio managers at hedge funds, an audited record of performance is standard. It's also common procedure for employees to disclose personal investments, although it's typically not part of the pre-screening process. Some choose to disclose this in advance if there is an obvious conflict of interest. For example, the hiring firm owns a majority interest in company A and the candidate is on the board of company A's biggest competitor.*

SC: Would you say a poor credit history is something that can make a break an offer, especially for a high level and high profile role, and especially if it came down to two candidates being neck-and-neck for the same role?

MK: *Depends on the role—but yes, having a poor credit history would put a candidate at a disadvantage.*

In December 2013, Senator Elizabeth Warren (D-Mass) proposed the Equal Employment Act, which was cosponsored by six fellow Democrats. If passed, the legislation "would effectively prohibit employers from requiring job applicants to disclose their credit history as part of the application process." Could this then mean that preemployment credit screening will soon be on the chopping block? I don't think so. Credit is still an equalizer, and keep in mind that employers aren't given nor are they concerned with credit scores but credit histories.

Warren said in a statement that the practice of checking job applicants' credit reports can create a vicious circle for poorer workers who fall into a financial hole and then are unable to procure the employment they need to dig themselves out. She argued that poor credit reports are often the result of unpaid medical bills, prolonged unemployment or even basic errors, which can be difficult to fix. She said these issues disproportionately affect poor and minority workers.

The Consumer Data Industry Association (CDIA), the trade association that represents the credit bureaus, had no official position on Warren's bill. Credit agencies have long insisted they don't sell credit scores for employment-screening purposes. They sell a modified version of your credit report, which contains detailed information about your credit history, but not your score. "Scores aren't used for employment in any way shape or form," said Norm Magnuson, vice president of public affairs at CDIA.

Magnuson said it's not minor information about how you pay your bills that employers are worried about, but serious red flags like tax liens or court judgments, which could show a pattern of irresponsible behavior. "So if you missed a few payments on your credit cards, they don't really care about that," Magnuson insisted. "What they do care about is that you have problems with the IRS, or if you have a bankruptcy. Those are pretty serious."

An employer must obtain permission from a job applicant to review his or her credit report and must inform the applicant if he or she was turned down because of something that appeared on the report. Applicants do have an opportunity to explain any known errors or delinquencies on their credit reports, but with the job market as competitive as it is, it's easy to imagine that an employer might choose an equally qualified candidate with an unblemished credit history.

A 2012 survey by the Society of Human Resources Management found that 47 percent of employers now use credit checks when hiring for some or all of the positions at their firms. Magnuson said it all comes down to the type of job you are seeking out—the more responsibility, the more likelihood a poor report could count against you. "If you apply to a bank as a teller, it's going to impact you if you have information like that on your credit report," he said.

Many workers' rights and privacy are likely to agree with Warren's bill. Sarah Ludwig, codirector of the Neighborhood Economic Development Advocacy Project (NEDAP), told the *New York Times* in March 2014 that many people denied employment because of a credit check are lower-wage workers applying to large retail chains.

As of this writing, the Equal Employment for All Act has been endorsed by more than 40 organizations, including NEDAP. In a statement, Sen. Warren said job seekers should be free to compete on their merits, not on whether they have enough money to pay their bills.[12]

CREDIT AND LOVE

Two people fall in love. Let's call them Blake and Ryan. They get serious and decide to get an apartment together that neither can really afford singly. They set up the cable, electric, and other utilities, some in one person's name, and some in the other's. To make things more convenient, they even set up a joint checking account together from which they can easily pay rent and bills.

Then one day, things go sour. Blake leaves, provides some money for remaining bills, and Ryan plans to stay until the apartment lease ends in five months. They discuss meeting at a later date, at the bank, to separate their names from or close their joint account. Then, Ryan loses his job.

Five months later Blake has a credit report pulled for a car loan preapproval, and he is more than surprised to discover a collection on his credit report. It's been filed by the former apartment's management company, and the amount is upward of $3,000. To make matters worse, every attempt at contacting Ryan has failed. And since the apartment lease was in both their names, as was their joint checking account, he's now on the hook for anything related to both.

When Blake checks the balance of their joint account which he knows he hasn't personally used since their breakup, he's shocked when he sees the account closed with an overdraft fee of $3,500. He looks at the account and transaction history and sees that, in addition to not stopping some of the auto payments that were going out to utility companies, Ryan also took out cash and bounced some rent checks.

Blake was never aware that the account had entered such a state of neglect. So now, in addition to having a massive collection on his credit report, Blake also runs the risk of having his name on bad terms with the bank and ChexSystems, jeopardizing his chances of opening new bank accounts in the future.

Wrecked by an Ex

If you think stories like Blake's and Ryan's above are outlandish and crazy, think again. Situations like these happen all the time, every day. I frequently heard stories like this when I was a loan originator. Time and time again, as I was reviewing credit reports with clients, I heard the anger (and sometimes tears) in their voices as they explained how they were wrecked by an ex, and why they were the victims of their vindictive or negligent partners' irresponsible financial habits. They felt blindsided, hung out to dry, taken advantage of, and worse, their credit had taken a beating because they had, in good faith, cosigned previous lease agreements, mortgage loans, credit cards bills, and utilities.

There is no explanation for peoples' behaviors when they are driven by anger, hurt, or sadness at the end of or many years after a relationship. We don't know if Ryan was a bad person or did those things intentionally; sometimes people just don't reach out for help and abandon everything. In some cases, when emotional trauma hits, a person may just give up on responsibilities, including the financial ones. Or it could be that they were never financially competent in the first place.

In cases of love and credit, I urge you to always, *always* put yourself first.

There are a lot of fish in the sea, and not all of them are raised with the same, if any, financial education. Basic money management skills are not taught in schools as part of the standard curriculum, so it's up to parents to introduce money concepts; otherwise they must be self-taught. I provide a lot of education resources on personal money management in the next Chapter, "Practice Makes Habit." If you want to brush up on your personal financial knowledge, know that it's never too late to learn and apply new skills.

Important Questions

When you consider the person with whom you're having a serious relationship—and with whom you could potentially be sharing your life, just consider these important questions about your partner's financial makeup:

- Do you know how they make money?
- Do you understand and respect their line of work?
- Do you have an idea of how much they make? (Not down to the penny, but a general idea)
- Does your partner respect money? Are they financially responsible or reckless in the way they manage personal finances such as rent, mortgages, bills, and other loans?
- Are your partner's spending behaviors confusing? Are you annoyed when they spend too much, or are overly frugal, cheap, or downright petty?
- Are you comfortable with the way your partner thinks about money? Do they constantly complain about not having any, or are they capable of earning it and thinking bigger picture?
- Are you comfortable with the way they discuss the subject in front of friends or family, and especially with you? In some cultures, discussing money is considered rude, whereas in others, money and business can dominate conversation.

There is no right or wrong answer to each one of the above questions. This is not a gauge for perfection because perfection doesn't exist. These questions are simply for you to form your own opinions and personal thresholds for the person with whom you're going to risk your greatest financial asset—your personal credit score. Use or sharpen your God-given, natural powers of observation. Open your eyes to your partners' behaviors when you're dating and address what makes you uncomfortable.

Ideally, the answers to the above questions can be answered because the two of you have discussed the subject, not because you've gone rooting around in their phone, personal laptop, or the trash bin.

Consider financial discussions to be the precursor to serious commitments such as marriage. Once you take those marital vows and enter into a legally binding courtship, it will be a lot harder after the fact to one day stumble upon your spouse's unsavory financial behaviors.

Working as a team is a beautiful thing—it not only provides the foundation for a strong union, but it's also an empowering step to take together. Who will manage the bills? The investments? At the very least, you want your biggest supporter in love and life to be on your team.

A Good Credit/Bad Credit Partnership

If you've got excellent credit and your partner doesn't, then consider how you may be compassionate and supportive of the work that lies ahead. Help keep your partner's eye on the prize. Consider the time and effort involved in improving and repairing credit, and offer to lend a helping hand. Use this book and the tools recommended to help your partner repair and maintain good credit.

When you enter into a serious relationship with someone, decide if their past financial behavior is something you can tolerate or help them weather. As a couple, the combined strength of two excellent credit scores will certainly make life a lot easier than if you are constantly struggling or worse, if you resent your loved one because of a poor credit situation.

Be Advised, Some People Never Change

True, you may love that person with all your heart, but you've also got to understand that it will require a serious change of attitude and unlearned behaviors for any sort of change. Many times people can learn from mistakes and change their behaviors. Only time will tell whether some people want the help or just can't be helped. It starts with them. Sometimes the sad reality is that many people *won't* change.

If you've got bad credit and your partner doesn't, then make sure they understand why your current situation exists and what you'd like to do about improving it. Being aloof and nonchalant won't likely put you in their good graces, nor will it provide them very much faith that you can be a financially successful team. If you're serious about your relationship, then you'll commit to improve your credit with this book and the recommended tools inside. If *both* of you have credit issues and commit to working on improvement together, than revisit Chapter 2 on ways to get focused and committed and start on the rewarding journey of credit cleanup. It can be a worthy goal with a lot of satisfaction at the end.

Marriage, Divorce, and Credit

No situation is more damaging to credit than when a couple with joint debts and assets splits, and someone gets nasty. Ideally both parties will be mature and tie up loose ends in a civil manner. But at times, people act with malicious intent or out of spiteful revenge whereas others may just be habitually late with managing timely payments. When this happens postdivorce, credit can suffer as a result.

Unfortunately, according to our bankruptcy trustee Chris Welker, "The most common cause of personal financial problems is marital and relationship breakdown. If you think about a couple who is acting responsibly, they are paying their bills and their incomes are sufficient to cover all of their living expenses. Now imagine if this couple separates. They have no additional income as the result of the separation, but their living expenses will instantly double, not to mention the costs associated with separation." This can certainly be a financially straining situation indeed, and many partners will seek additional alimony or child support if they aren't working.

Homes and Mortgages

In cases of divorce where a couple shared a house and a mortgage, one resolution is to sell the home, which will eventually pay off the joint mortgage. Until the house is sold, the parties can decide who pays the mortgage and how. After the house is sold, any proceeds can be split after the mortgage is paid, and life goes on.

In most cases though, especially when there are children involved, one side is likely to stay in the house while the other moves out. In this case the person remaining in the house will be given a certain timeline to refinance the mortgage out of the other party's name entirely.

In some cases the person remaining in the house cannot qualify with sufficient income or credit to refinance the mortgage on their own. In these cases, the other party must set some terms and decide how long they're willing to remain on the loan. Here, Liz Weston provides the following advice:

If your ex wants to continue living in the family home with your kids, you might agree that the house will be sold when the youngest is 18. Make sure this agreement is part of your divorce decree, and ask the lender to send loan statements and coupons so that you can make sure the loan is getting paid. At the very least, you should be able to get Internet or phone access to the account so that you can monitor the situation.

If you're already divorced, you might still want to get access to the account and make the payments if your ex is falling behind. Again, your divorce decree might allow you to take your ex back to court for reimbursement. If your ex could refinance but won't, you might have to resort to bribes—a cash payment or more time with the kids in exchange for getting a new loan.[13]

It is ill-advised for the person moving out to sign over any property ownership or title rights, known as a quitclaim deed, *before* the mortgage is refinanced out of their name. By doing so, they are opening themselves up to risk, since they'll be on the hook for a lien to a property to which they have no ownership. Even worse, if the other party defaults on the mortgage, they'll have their credit damaged for a mortgage on a property they no longer own.

In all cases, a divorce attorney should be consulted to provide more clarity in these situations because the details on property, liens, mortgages, title, and ownership can be hairy and vary by state.

Credit Cards

As long as your ex is tied to any of your credit card accounts, you are on the hook for their purchasing behavior. Determine which credit cards you've allowed your ex to use as joint account holder or as an authorized user. Then, call the credit card companies to have their name removed and cards canceled. If a large part of any remaining credit card balances is primarily due to an ex's purchases, then a divorce decree may allow for a transfer of a certain portion of balances to be moved or paid for by the ex. Again, a divorce attorney should be consulted in these matters.

Proactive, Not Reactive: Getting a Prenuptial Agreement

During the premarital bliss and excitement, the last thing you want to discuss with your future spouse is the ultimate mood killer: the prenuptial agreement. While the idea of having one may just be downright unromantic, consider it a must if either of you is entering into the marriage with any of the following that you can call your own:

1. Job
2. House (or any other property such as a boat, motorcycle, or real estate)

3. Car(s)

4. Business

5. Credit Cards

6. Liquid assets (savings and retirement accounts).

The simple reality is that in the United States 41 percent of marriages these days end in divorce,[14] and this percentage goes higher or lower, depending on age and socioeconomic conditions. You don't want your hard-earned items being contested if divorce happens. A prenuptial agreement simply clarifies ownership and assets, stipulating what's yours prior to marriage. That way, in the event of divorce, these terms can be revisited in case an ex makes any claims to items such as credit cards, property, business proceeds, holdings, and other items that were solely your responsibility before the marriage.

Also, let me say this (especially to women): There is no reason to be offended if your partner brings up a prenuptial agreement. A marriage is a merger of assets, and if you have any of the six items in the above list then you bring up the conversation *first*. Protect yourself and all that you've worked hard for.

You'll have to consult a divorce attorney for prenuptial agreements. Hope for the best, prepare for the worst. You'll be glad you did.

Keep It All in One Place

Nowadays, with as many women in the workplace making as much money as men and buying as many properties as men,[15] there are no prescribed roles for who is expected to manage the finances; it can be either person in the relationship.

If one person typically manages the finances in the household—the payment of bills, the accounts, the investments, and more, then that person should be comfortable putting all of these items in a secure spreadsheet (in an encrypted file, on Dropbox or password-protected Evernote, the tools referenced in Chapter 2, "Getting Prepared") or worksheet and telling the other person where this list is kept. All credit cards, all account information, all property tax and insurance contacts, even details for any automobiles in the family should be logged, or even one step further, provided to an executor of your estate, your estate attorney, or personal lawyer.

If things are managed online, then by all means provide the user log-in credentials for the other person as well. Could you imagine what would happen to your partner if one day, God forbid something happened to you, the financial manager of the household, and you weren't around to handle everything? Imagine the stressful image of your loved one trying to navigate through even the most basic of your financials. *Don't* leave them in that situation.

A Last Word

For all of you singletons out there, remember our executive coach, Jason Womack, from Chapter 2? He said, "Change who you spend your life with, and your life will change." Perhaps you've gone through the experience of being in a relationship where you were more credit responsible than your ex. Or perhaps you were in a relationship where you had no clue as to your ex-partner's personal financial situation and felt as if everything was kept under a veil of secrecy. A true partnership involves total financial disclosure.

Credit and money behavior is important when considering your partner in life. It may not be a deal breaker, but that's something you'll have to decide for yourself.

NINE

Practice Makes Habit

First of all, the concept of perfection is great, but nonexistent. No one is perfect, and what I'd like to believe is that by implementing good credit behaviors and *practice*, we can make this our *habit* to do only that.

The author, trader, investor, and entrepreneur, James Altucher, in his book *Choose Yourself* said, "It's your best thinking that got you here."

So if you're not happy about your current financial situation, then it's time to change your best thinking toward the credit and money management skills that got you to where you are today.

As you grow and your life changes, your personal financial circumstances change, as do the financial risks that you can tolerate. Perhaps you were more responsible in your twenties than thirties, or vice versa. Perhaps major life events such as marriage, divorce, unemployment, medical hardships, or looking after your family members has impacted you, and you are ready to focus on your personal situation again—no one else's but yours. It's *your* life, and you deserve that much, right?

Understand this: Good or bad, your credit status is not permanent. While companies and lenders may judge you by a credit score, don't judge yourself by it. This book has provided knowledge for ways to improve your credit score, and if you apply it, then you will always be able to be in control of where you stand.

A poor credit score is not the *only* consequence of poor money management. Excellent credit can disappear in a swoop. Miss a payment here or there, lose your job, or have an emergency that requires drawing up credit card balances, and you will be glad you had the excellent credit in your past to fall back on as a security blanket. Poor credit is not a permanent situation, but it *does* require action, energy, and time on your part to reverse it. In addition to the tips throughout this book and especially in Chapter 6, "Improving Your Credit Score," during the writing of this book I wanted to also share my latest discoveries in budget and money management apps and tools. All of these combine to enable you to have control over your money and best of all, know where you stand.

POSITIVE CREDIT AND MONEY BEHAVIORS

A budget means having a clear realization of how much money is coming in minus how much and where the money is going out. Think of it as a big funnel, where money goes in at the top, and the cinched part in the middle is where you're tightening and allocating what goes out and where at the bottom.

For some this may be fairly basic, but for others I know it will be pretty overwhelming to all of a sudden be thinking about a budget and your credit on a daily, weekly, or monthly basis, especially if it's not something you actively thought about before. And I know it's equally as challenging mentally to rethink the way you've managed your money if you haven't been so responsible or detailed about it in the past.

Plenty of financial management gurus espouse their advice and systems to be the best. While each of their ideas may work, it's time-consuming to sift out what works and what doesn't. It's easy to get lost in the noise.

My advice is to keep it simple for starters, and set up a system that works *for you*. Don't overwhelm yourself trying to figure out a budget so much that you give up—that defeats the purpose of all the reading and hard work you've done so far.

I'll be the first to admit that I am sometimes easily distracted and have a bit of shiny object syndrome when it comes to seeing and reading or being told, shared, and tweeted about the latest big thing, apps, or website.

In the old days, when I didn't have a slew of automated tools at my disposal, I managed my budget at the basest level with an Excel spreadsheet. Every month I gathered my documents and input data into this spreadsheet—where the x-axis columns represented each month of the year, and the y-axis columns listed each category of bill payment for monies sent out. And of course there were formulas peppered throughout to account for debits and credits to reconcile monthly ending balances.

I look back at my young self and if I could speak to her today, I'd say, "Girl, why are you not paying someone to do this for you. You should be out enjoying the fruits of your labor and having fun, not sitting here poring away over some spreadsheet!"

Truth is, I enjoyed geeking out over this kind of stuff and this monthly practice of reconciling my debits and credits, for some reason, crystallized my budget in my head—and suddenly my outgoings, dollar for dollar, became very real and tangible.

Some people grasp concepts visually, while others prefer more linear presentations. In creative or technology industries, a written treatment or proposal may also be supported by a diagram, wire frame, mindmap, storyboard—you name it. The spreadsheet provided a linear view, which I could also convert into a visual graph if I desired. Either way, once I understood the magnitude of my budget, I was able to wholly sense what required attention.

Luckily, technology has come full circle when it comes to tracking and making you aware of your incomings and outgoings and getting your budget under control.

THE LATEST AND GREATEST APPS AND TOOLS

Just like you pulled your credit report to see where you stood credit wise, you may need some help getting an idea of where you stand money wise. As I mentioned, lucky for us that there are innovative new companies that are revolutionizing the way you think about your money. And there are few feelings in this world that rank higher than the feeling of being empowered over your money.

Here are a few of my new favorites:

Simple

Based in Portland, Oregon, Simple (simple.com) aims to make banking and budgeting its namesake. I'm a customer myself and was so in the company's invitation-only, beta phase.

Simple operates as a digital bank and equips clients with a debit card—a super-sleek, all-white card at that. If there were a design competition for consumer debit and credit cards, this card and the American Express Black Centurion card would win, respectively. As a sucker for design I believe in all things, well, *simple.*

When you open your Simple account you can fund it by linking any external checking or savings accounts, or by setting it up for employer direct deposit.

A Digital Bank

For those of you who may feel uneasy about moving your funds away from a brick-and-mortar institution and into a digital bank, rest assured I myself overcame this fear when I opened a digital savings account back in 2007 with what was then ING Bank (now Capital One 360). Fearing the unknown, my heart was racing as I clicked to confirm a transfer of funds from a Bank of America savings account over to an ING account that was yielding a much higher APR. And it was painless. To me, my money was all in a nebulous, electronic cloud anyway. If you're still feeling squirrely about it, keep in mind that the Federal Deposit Insurance Corporation (FDIC) insures deposits and funds up to $250,000 at legitimate banks and financial institutions.

Back to Simple. The beauty of it comes alive when your spending is tracked by Simple's software. Your spending behaviors come to life. You can follow along online, or through the Simple app, which is available in both Apple iOS and Android operating systems.

When I spoke to Krista Berlincourt, Simple's Head of Communications, she indicated that the company's approach to banking, budgeting, and financial management emphasizes a client's mindfulness toward his or her money.

Where there's always been a specter of wrongdoing and penalties the minute you do something wrong with your banking accounts, like missing a bill payment, or accidentally overdrafting—Simple makes it easier to stay on track.

Demystifying What's Safe to Spend

Customers aren't shamed in case they make a minor error—Simple doesn't charge overdraft fees, nor fees for going below some arbitrary balance. And unlike most banks with a confusing "Available Balance" number that may not take into account your most recent transactions (or even future payments and earmarked savings), Simple clearly defines what portion of your money is actually available with a unique feature called "Safe-to-Spend." The Safe-to-Spend amount is clearly indicated, for example when viewing a Simple account online (Figure 9.1).

Another of Simple's exemplary features? You can set up goals from within a single account, rather than create multiple savings accounts. Then, save and contribute toward your goals—whether immediately or over time. You're also able to spend *from* a goal, which is all reflected in your Safe-to-Spend amount. This way, you'll never feel like you're

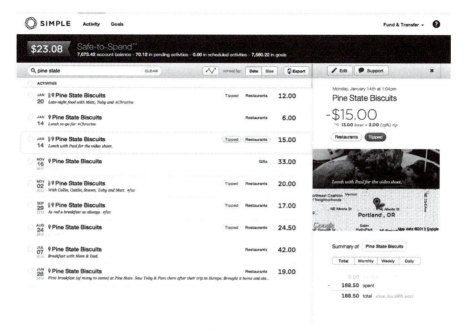

Figure 9.1   Simple Safe-to-Spend® Overview

juggling and anticipating your bank balance's movements. Once you earmark funds for goals, voila—the software allocates money where you want it to go.

This is incredibly helpful for a traveler on the road or even for business budgeting. Simple even allows you to append tags, hashtags, notes and pictures to your transactions. This helps customers create a spending story through transactions, and easily locate, track, and sort expenses. You could prepare for taxes by adding *#deductible* to relevant personal or work transactions, in real time. You could even add *#Starbucks*, or *#coffee* or *#businessmeetings*, to keep track of your morning cuppas and business pow-wows.

No More Mental Arithmetic

When I spoke with Simple's CEO, Josh Reich, he drove this point home: "If you don't have a clear understanding of where you stand, you're never *really* going to be able to stay on top of your finances." An Australian who relocated to the United States, Josh's vision for Simple came from being disenchanted with the American banking system and feeling like he was constantly fighting with his banks.

If there was a changing due date on a bill, I felt like it had caught me off guard. I felt, 'Why do I have to be on top of so many things to take care of my *own* money?' The bank made it *my* problem.

Fundamentally, massive banks make money by keeping their customers confused—overdrafts (make) *so* much money for them! Here you are with this $2,000 computer in front of you, and you're expected to do mental arithmetic, which the bank doesn't want to do for you.

So he and cofounder Shamir Karkal created Simple to do just that. "We're going to flip the banking business model upside down and return it to where banks make money by earning it, not depending on fee revenue. We're providing tools to spend smarter and save more, not on glitzy marketing campaigns, and we think consumers will appreciate that," Josh said.

As of this writing, Simple had processed roughly $6 million in transactions with $1.7 trillion transferred in from user accounts.

As they grow, they'll continue to roll out new features. When I spoke with Josh, he'd just paid Shamir for lunch using a new "Simple instant" feature, which mimics Venmo's peer-to-peer payments system in its ability for accountholders to pay each other easily.

Mint

Mint (mint.com) continues to be a popular web-based, budget, and financial management software. It's a free tool that was sold to Intuit, the behemoth behind TurboTax, and takes the guesswork out of where your money's going every month. You can synch all of your bank accounts and monthly bills, and since Mint is only a money-tracking and analyzing tool, money can never go in or out.

Mint is great if you want one place to review your overall net assets, since you can compare your debts to your overall liquid assets, and see where you stand month to month. If you have the patience to set up your account and categorize monthly line items, you'll find it to be a functional, basic budgeting tool. In my experience, categorizing is the painful part; from there you can decide whether Mint's tools work for you. Mint's app, Mint Quickview, made the AppStore's "Best of 2012" list and provides the same categorization and snapshot features of the web tool.

Moneytrackin'

Moneytrackin' (moneytrackin.com) is a free online web app that allows you to track all your expenses and income easily. It intends to be a simple yet powerful online budget management tool that offers a clear view of your financial situation. One interesting feature of Moneytrackin' is sharing and collaboration. If you are working with a family member or your roommate to keep budgets in line, you can do so with ease and work together on the same account to reach financial goals.[1]

BillGuard

BillGuard (billguard.com) allows you to quickly see balances and charges across all your credit and debit cards. A worthy Mint competitor in the budget management space, BillGuard also features more granular spending analytics and has community-powered reconciliation, which clears up vague merchant transactions. For example, if one user provides input that "Lily Kate St. Louis LLC" is actually "Lily's Boutique" then the records matching those transactions will be reconciled across user accounts. BillGuard also claims to be the number one "grey charge" (as mentioned in Chapter 3) preventer by alerting you of unwanted and deceptive subscription-type fees.

Check

Check's (check.me) iOS and Android app reminds you when your bills are due, so you can keep them paid on time. Paying bills timely is one of the top ways to improve your credit score, as mentioned in Chapter 6. You can also securely link your bank accounts and schedule outgoing bill payments, directly from the app.

For Small Business Owners and Entrepreneurs

Outright

For entrepreneurs and small business owners, Outright (outright.com) gets rid of tedious bookkeeping and data entry processes. Considered a basic alternative to the more sophisticated QuickBooks, and especially great for help with PayPal bookkeeping, Outright records and organizes all your income and expenses. Come tax time, you can worry less about accurate payments and deductions. It's also free to use unless you want annual and quarterly reports for tax purposes, in which case as of this writing it costs $9.95 monthly. With this software it's likely your numbers will be more accurate, you'll see more deductions, and you won't pay more taxes than you have to.

inDinero

inDinero (indinero.com) helps to integrate and manage all business accounts on an intuitive online dashboard. inDinero claims to help slash unnecessary costs, collect payments faster from customers, and show you which of your products and services are earning you the most money.

Educational Resources

Kahn Academy

One corporate bank is trying to instill "Better Money Habits" for its clients. That bank is Bank of America, who partnered with Salman Khan of Khan Academy, a highly respected online educator, to educate clients and prospective customers on the basics of money management. When asked to grade their knowledge of personal finance, 40 percent of American adults who participated in the National Foundation of Credit Counseling's 2013 Financial Literacy Survey gave themselves a grade of C, D, or F.[2]

The educational videos at kahnacademy.org already feature tutorials for math from basic grade level up to high school calculus, science, history, and art history. They also collaborate with art museums and offer college test prep and a number of topics on economics for kids and adults alike.

The videos at bettermoneyhabits.com feature the same variety of white-board-style, conversational, straightforward, and accessible guidance. As of this writing, there were several credit-related videos, such as "Understanding Credit," "How Credit Scores Affect Interest Rates," and "How is Credit Card Interest Calculated," but it's certainly worth a look to learn more about the many other topics on personal finance.

Investing

Betterment

If you've got money to invest, and want to get into the investment game, or just find investing a loaded chore, Betterment (betterment.com) may be a great introduction to personal financial investment. Betterment acts as a virtual financial planner and makes investing simple, by allocating your funds for you into a short-listed group of handpicked, goal-based accounts based on proprietary software. It's a "set it and forget it" methodology with advice, automation, and accessibility. Betterment has a simple all-inclusive management fee as low as 0.15 percent, and you can view your accounts online or with its app.

Wikinvest

If you have investments such as a 401k, brokerage, and other financial accounts with a wealth manager, Wikinvest (wikinvest.com)—no relation to Wikipedia—finally enables you to merge those investments together into one manageable dashboard. They'll send you a weekly e-mail as well, charting your combined portfolio's weekly performance. I can't tell you how fantastic this is, instead of logging in to various accounts to look at your investment balances. On top of that, it has a community-sourced team of contributors that provide neutral to bullish commentary, much like the diverse news and insights you'll find from Seeking Alpha (seekingalpha.com). There's also a Money School section on the site, which has great articles ranging in topics like personal finance, investing, retirement, and taxes.

ENDNOTES

Get on Track with Positive Credit Management Behaviors

At the start of this book, I told you I was dedicated to helping you improve your credit score. I hope that by now you've understood why your credit score is your greatest financial asset, and that you've found the knowledge and tips throughout this book helpful and actionable along the way.

Credit management doesn't stop with fixing the inaccurate or damaged parts as a result of past behaviors and circumstances. We've been largely *reactive* to our scores. Now, we've got to be *proactive* and nurture our credit and money behaviors. Trust me, it takes much more work to repair poor credit than applying a daily practice nurture and prevention.

I want you to have a sense of control and implement what works best for you. I want you to always, at any given time, know where you stand. What I don't want is for you to have any more surprises when you go to apply for an apartment lease, cable or cell phone service, a job, a new car lease or loan, and lastly, a home loan. As long as you are aware and stick to the tips and apply the knowledge, you're on your way to improving your credit score, your greatest asset.

I want to hear your stories. Please go to the online companion to The *Credit Cleanup Book* (tccbonline.com), drop me a line, say Hi, and most of all, submit your stories of credit cleanup. I may share them with the world! After all, I take inspiration from everyone, everywhere.

Here's to you and your greatest financial asset—your credit score.

Notes

PREFACE

1. John Maxfield, "5 Biggest Mortgage Originators in America," The Motley Fool, http://www.fool.com/investing/general/2013/09/15/5-biggest-mortgage-lenders-in-america.aspx (accessed March 29, 2014).

2. Kara Scannell and Camilla Hall, "BofA in $9.5bn Settlement with Regulator," *Financial Times*, http://www.ft.com/intl/cms/s/0/07697b7c-b534-11e3-a746-00144feabdc0.html?siteedition=intl (accessed March 29, 2014).

CHAPTER 1

1. Caroline Salas Gage, "Household Borrowing Rises Most in Six Years in NY Fed Report," Bloomberg.com, http://www.bloomberg.com/news/2014-02-18/household-debt-in-u-s-climbs-most-in-six-years-in-ny-fed-survey.html (accessed March 29, 2014).

2. Malgorzata Wozniacka and Snigdha Sen, "Credit Scores—What You Should Know about Your Own," PBS, http://www.pbs.org/wgbh/pages/frontline/shows/credit/more/scores.html (accessed March 29, 2014).

3. "History," Experian PLC, http://www.experianplc.com/about-experian/history.aspx (accessed March 29, 2014).

4. "The Fair Credit Reporting Act (FCRA) and the Privacy of Your Credit Report," EPIC, http://epic.org/privacy/fcra/ (accessed March 29, 2014).

5. Liz Pulliam Weston, *Your Credit Score: Your Money & What's at Stake* (Upper Saddle River: FT Press, 2010).

6. "About Innovis," Innovis, https://www.innovis.com/InnovisWeb/aboutInnovis.html (accessed March 29, 2014).

7. "The Fair Credit Reporting Act (FCRA) and the Privacy of Your Credit Report," EPIC, http://epic.org/privacy/fcra/ (accessed March 29, 2014).

8. Ibid.

9. "Credit Reporting," Federal Trade Commission, http://www.ftc.gov/news-events/media-resources/consumer-finance/credit-reporting (accessed March 29, 2014).

10. "Credit Crisis," Investopedia, http://www.investopedia.com/terms/c/credit-crisis.asp (accessed March 28, 2014).

11. "About Us," Consumer Financial Protection Bureau, http://www.consumerfinance.gov/the-bureau/ (accessed March 31, 2014).

12. "CFPB Bulletin 2011–05 (Enforcement and Fair Lending)," CFPB, http://files.consumerfinance.gov/f/2011/12/CFPB_Enforcement_Bulletin_12-15-11.pdf (accessed March 29, 2014).

13. Dana Neal, *Best Credit: How to Win the Credit Game* (Boulder: Paladin Press, 2006).

CHAPTER 2

1. Jason Womack, *Your Best Just Got Better* (Hoboken: John Wiley & Sons, 2012).

2. Jim Hartness and Neil Eskelin, *The 24 Hour Turnaround: Use 24 One-Hour Time Periods to Turn Your Life Around* (Revell, 2002).

CHAPTER 3

1. Dan Rafter, "Paying These Bills on Time? Credit Bureaus Don't Care," Fox Business, http://www.foxbusiness.com/personal-finance/2013/12/09/paying-these-bills-on-time-credit-bureaus-dont-care/?intcmp=related (accessed March 29, 2014).

2. "Grey Charges in America," BillGuard, https://www.billguard.com/greycharges (last accessed March 31, 2014).

3. "Creditscore.com Review," Review, http://www.reviews.com/credit-report/creditscorecom/ (accessed March 29, 2014).

4. Mandi Woodruff, "There's No Reason to Pay for Your Credit Score Anymore," Business Insider, http://www.businessinsider.com/credit-sesame-credit-karma-free-credit-scores-2013-9 (accessed March 29, 2014).

5. TechCrunch Disrupt is a technology conference created by the online tech journal, techcrunch.com. At its highly anticipated conferences

in major cities around the world, participants create products at 24-hour hackathons, a shortlist of the latest and greatest startup companies pitch to panels and an audience of potential seed investors and venture capitalists.

CHAPTER 4

1. "Understanding Your FICO Score," myFICO, http://www.myfico .com/Downloads/Files/myFICO_UYFS_Booklet.pdf (accessed March 29, 2014).

2. "Analysis of Differences between Consumer- and Creditor-Purchased Credit Scored," CFPB, http://files.consumerfinance.gov/f/201209_Analy sis_Differences_Consumer_Credit.pdf (accessed March 29, 2014).

3. "FICO Delinquency Chances 2008," Blogspot, http://1.bp.blogspot .com/_5aAsxFJOeMw/SO2AB06ig5I/AAAAAAAABSw/rQfEih8liUc /s400/FICOdelinquencyChances2008.jpg (accessed March 29, 2014).

4. Frederic Huynh, "US Credit Quality Continues to Inch Forward— Banking Analytics Blog," Banking Analytics Blog, http://bankinganaly ticsblog.fico.com/2014/02/us-credit-quality-continues-to-inch-forward .html (accessed March 29, 2014).

5. Dana Neal, *Best Credit: How to Win the Credit Game* (Boulder: Paladin Press, 2006).

6. Ibid.

7. Ibid.

8. "Prescreened Credit and Insurance Offers," Federal Trade Commission, https://www.consumer.ftc.gov/articles/0148-prescreened-credit-and-insurance-offers (accessed March 29, 2014).

CHAPTER 5

1. Dana Neal, *Best Credit: How to Win the Credit Game* (Boulder: Paladin Press, 2006).

2. Ibid.

3. Kelly Dilworth, "Ten Surefire Steps to Get Errors off Your Credit Reports," Fox Business, http://www.foxbusiness.com/personal-finance/2012/10/03/10-surefire-steps-to-get-errors-off-your-credit-reports/ (accessed March 29, 2014).

4. Gregory Karp, "Give Yourself Some Credit," *Chicago Tribune*, http://articles.chicagotribune.com/2012-07-20/site/sc-cons-0719-karp spend-20120720_1_free-report-credit-reports-dispute-errors (accessed March 29, 2014).

5. Liz Pulliam Weston, *Your Credit Score: Your Money & What's at Stake* (Upper Saddle River: FT Press, 2010).

CHAPTER 6

1. Dana Neal, *Best Credit: How to Win the Credit Game* (Boulder: Paladin Press, 2006).

2. John Sileo, "Top Five Reasons for Corporations to Educate Employees on Identity Theft," All Business, http://www.allbusiness.com/crime-law-enforcement-corrections/criminal-offenses-fraud/12585315-1.html (accessed March 29, 2014).

3. "Check Fraud Prevention," National Check Fraud Center, http://www.ckfraud.org/ckfraud.html (accessed March 27, 2014).

4. "Bank Account Opening Assessment Tools: ChexSystems and More," Credit Builders Alliance, http://creditbuildersalliance.org/whats-new/resources/bank-account-opening-assessment-tools-chexsystems-and-more (accessed March 29, 2014).

5. Blake Ellis, "Denied a Bank Account? You Have Options," CNNMoney, http://money.cnn.com/2012/08/16/pf/second-chance-checking/ (accessed March 29, 2014).

6. Ibid.

CHAPTER 7

1. "Strategies for Getting Out of Debt," Welker & Associates Inc., http://welker.ca/blog/post/strategies-getting-out-debt (accessed March 29, 2014).

2. "Credit Cards: Should I Pay Down My Mortgage or Pay Off My Credit Card?," Quora, http://www.quora.com/Credit-Cards/Should-I-pay-down-my-mortgage-or-pay-off-my-credit-card (accessed March 29, 2014).

3. "Coping with Debt," Federal Trade Commission, http://www.consumer.ftc.gov/articles/0150-coping-debt (accessed March 29, 2014).

4. Allie Johnson, "Do You Have What It Takes for DIY Debt Settlement?," Fox Business, http://www.foxbusiness.com/personal-finance/2014/01/29/do-have-what-it-takes-for-diy-debt-settlement/ (accessed March 29, 2014).

5. Ibid.

6. "Debt Collection," Federal Trade Commission, http://www.consumer.ftc.gov/articles/0149-debt-collection (accessed March 29, 2014).

7. Dana Neal, *Best Credit: How to Win the Credit Game* (Boulder: Paladin Press, 2006).

8. See note 6.

9. See note 7.

10. "Student Loan Debt Statistics," American Student Assistance, http://www.asa.org/policy/resources/stats/ (accessed March 29, 2014).

11. Meta Brown, Andrew Haughwout, Donghoon Lee, Maricar Mabutas, and Wilbert van der Klaauw, "Grading Student Loans," Liberty Street Economics, http://libertystreeteconomics.newyorkfed.org/2012/03/grading-student-loans.html (accessed March 29, 2014).

12. Rohit Chopra, "Too Big to Fail: Student Debt Hits a Trillion," Consumer Financial Protection Bureau, http://www.consumerfinance.gov/blog/too-big-to-fail-student-debt-hits-a-trillion/ (accessed March 29, 2014).

13. "Grading Student Loans," Federal Reserve Bank of New York, http://libertystreeteconomics.newyorkfed.org/2012/03/grading-student-loans.html (accessed March 31, 2014).

14. The White House, "We Can't Wait: Obama Administration to Lower Student Loan Payments for Millions of Borrowers," The White House, http://www.whitehouse.gov/the-press-office/2011/10/25/we-cant-wait-obama-administration-lower-student-loan-payments-millions-b (accessed March 29, 2014).

15. See note 13.

16. "Federal Student Loan Programs—Overview," New America Foundation, http://febp.newamerica.net/background-analysis/federal-student-loan-programs-overview (accessed March 29, 2014).

17. Rachel Rowan, "Last Ditch Student Loan Measures—How to Choose Deferment vs Forbearance," Tuition Blog, http://www.tuition.io/blog/2013/05/last-ditch-student-loan-measures-how-to-choose-deferment-vs-forbearance/ (accessed March 29, 2014).

CHAPTER 8

1. Diana Olick, "Will the American Dream Still Include Owning a Home?," CNBC, http://www.cnbc.com/id/101479780 (accessed March 29, 2014).

2. Prashant Gopal and John Gittelsohn, "Americans Shut Out of Home Market Threaten Recovery: Mortgages," Bloomberg, http://www.bloomberg.com/news/2014-03-05/americans-shut-out-of-home-market-threaten-recovery-mortgages.html (accessed March 29, 2014).

3. Diana Olick, "Will the American Dream Still Include Owning a Home?," CNBC, http://www.cnbc.com/id/101479780 (accessed March 29, 2014).

4. Ibid.

5. "Housing Price Conundrum (Part 2)," Khan Academy, https://www.khanacademy.org/economics-finance-domain/core-finance/housing/housing-price-conundrum/v/housing-price-conundrum--part-2 (accessed March 29, 2014).

6. Rates tied to the one-month or six-month adjusting LIBOR, or "London Interbank Offered Rate" index.

7. "Qualified Mortgage Definition for HUD Insured or Guaranteed Single Family Mortgages," Department of Housing and Urban Development, http://portal.hud.gov/hudportal/documents/huddoc?id=QMProposedRule.pdf (accessed March 31, 2014).

8. Dewan, Shaila, "In Home Loans, Subprime Faces as a Dirty Word." *The New York Times*, June 29, 2014. Front Page.

9. Heidi Evans, "Accion USA Micro-Lending Organization Aids Immigrants, Women and Minority Small-Business Owners," New York Daily News, http://www.nydailynews.com/new-york/uptown/accion-usa-micro-lending-organization-aids-immigrants-women-minority-small-business-owners-article-1.116856 (March 31, 2014).

10. Karen E Klein, "Funding a New Small Business? Don't Bother with Banks," Bloomberg Businessweek Small Business, http://www.businessweek.com/articles/2014-02-13/funding-a-new-small-business-dont-bother-with-banks (accessed March 31, 2014).

11. In 2008, federal authorities arrested Bernard P. Madoff in what was revealed as the largest Ponzi scheme in history. A Ponzi scheme is a form of fraud where investors in an enterprise are paid with returns from the money invested by other, and usually later investors, rather than the true dividends earned by their own investment. The scheme was named after Charles Ponzi (d. 1949) who carried out such fraud in 1919–20.

12. Christopher Kara, "Elizabeth Warren Takes on Pre-Employment Credit Checks, But Bill Faces Strong Industry Opposition," International Business Times, http://www.ibtimes.com/elizabeth-warren-takes-pre-employment-credit-checks-bill-faces-strong-industry-opposition-1514384 (accessed March 29, 2014).

13. Liz Pulliam Weston, *Your Credit Score: Your Money & What's at Stake* (Upper Saddle River: FT Press, 2010).

14. "Divorce Rate," DivorceRate.Org, http://www.divorcerate.org/ (accessed March 31, 2014).

15. Susan Johnston, "More Single Women Buying Homes than Single Men," U.S. News and World Report, http://money.usnews.com/money/personal-finance/articles/2013/07/08/more-single-women-buying-homes-than-single-men (accessed March 31, 2014).

CHAPTER 9

1. Justin Stravarius, "12 Fantastic Finance Tracking & Management Apps," AppStorm, http://web.appstorm.net/roundups/finances-roundups/12-fantastic-finance-tracking-management-apps/ (accessed March 29, 2014).

2. "NFCC and NBPCA Financial Literacy Survey Reveals Consumers' Top Financial Concerns," NFCC, http://www.nfcc.org/newsroom/news releases/NFCC_NBPCA.cfm (accessed March 29, 2014).

Additional Resources

ARTICLES

Andriotis, AnnaMaria. "10 Things Credit Bureaus Won't Say." *MarketWatch*. http://www.marketwatch.com/story/10-things-credit-bureaus-wont-say-2013-02-15 (accessed July 3, 2014).

Detweiler, Gerri. "The Best Way to Consolidate Debt." *MarketWatch*. http://www.marketwatch.com/story/whats-the-best-way-to-consoli date-debt-2014-02-17 (accessed July 3, 2014).

Dzikowski, Patricia. "Negotiating on Credit Card Debt." http://www.nolo .com/legal-encyclopedia/negotiating-credit-card-debt.html (accessed July 3, 2014).

Federal Trade Commission. "Amended Free Credit Reports Rule Helps Consumers Avoid 'Free' Offers That Cost Money." http://www.ftc.gov /news-events/press-releases/2010/04/amended-free-credit-reports-rule-helps-consumers-avoid-free (accessed July 3, 2014).

Federal Trade Commission. "Consumer Information." *Credit Repair: How to Help Yourself*. http://www.consumer.ftc.gov/articles/0058-credit-repair-how-help-yourself (accessed July 3, 2014).

Federal Trade Commission. "Provisions of New Fair and Accurate Credit Transactions Act Will Help Reduce Identity Theft and Help Victims Recover: FTC." Federal Trade Commission. http://www.ftc.gov/news-events/press-releases/2004/06/provisions-new-fair-and-accurate-credit-transactions-act-will (accessed July 3, 2014).

Howard, Clark. "Paying Off Credit Card Debt." *Clark Howard: Save More, Spend Less and Avoid Rip-offs*. http://www.clarkhoward.com

/news/clark-howard/personal-finance-credit/paying-off-credit-card-debt/nFbH/ (accessed July 3, 2014).

Morales, Tatiana. "Understanding Your Credit Score." *CBSNews*. http://www.cbsnews.com/news/understanding-your-credit-score/ (accessed July 3, 2014).

Obringer, Lee Ann. "How Credit Reports Work." *HowStuffWorks*. http://money.howstuffworks.com/personal-finance/debt-management/credit-report.htm (accessed July 3, 2014).

Orman, Suze. "Get Your FICO Score." http://apps.suzeorman.com/igsbase/igstemplate.cfm?SRC=MD012&SRCN=aoedetails&GnavID=84&SnavID=20&TnavID=&AreasofExpertiseID=20 (accessed July 3, 2014).

Weston, Liz. "9 Fast Fixes for Your Credit Scores." *MSNMoney*. http://money.msn.com/credit-rating/9-fast-fixes-for-your-credit-scores-liz-weston?wvsessionid=60e0f518e1e04530bf2000841f758089 (accessed July 3, 2014).

ARTICLES AVAILABLE AT WWW.MYFICO.COM

"About Credit Reports." *Your Credit Report: What's in It & How It's Used by Lenders*. http://www.myfico.com/CreditEducation/CreditReports.aspx (accessed July 3, 2014).

"Credit Applications: Know My Rights." *Applying for Credit: Know Your Rights*. http://www.myfico.com/CreditEducation/Rights/CreditApplicationRights.aspx (accessed July 3, 2014).

"Credit Billing & EFT Statements: Know My Rights." *Unauthorized Electronic Fund Transfers: Your Rights under FCBA*. http://www.myfico.com/CreditEducation/Rights/CreditStatementRights.aspx (accessed July 3, 2014).

"Credit Bureau Investigation: What If I Disagree?" Credit Bureau Investigation. http://www.myfico.com/CreditEducation/Rights/InvestigationDisagree.aspx (accessed July 3, 2014).

"Credit Checks & Inquiries." *Credit Checks: How Credit Report Inquiries Affect Your Credit Score*. http://www.myfico.com/CreditEducation/CreditChecks/Inquiries.aspx (accessed July 3, 2014).

"Credit Reports: Know My Rights." *Credit Applications*. http://www.myfico.com/CreditEducation/Rights/CreditReportRights.aspx (accessed July 3, 2014).

"Credit Score Facts & Fallacies." *Credit Score Facts & Fallacies: The Truth Behind Common Myths*. http://www.myfico.com/CreditEducation/FactsFallacies.aspx (accessed July 3, 2014).

"Debt & Debt Collectors: Know My Rights." *Help with Debt Collectors: Know Your Rights and Obligations*. http://www.myfico.com/CreditEducation/Rights/DebtRights.aspx (accessed July 3, 2014).

"Fixing Credit Report Errors: What to Do." *Fixing Credit Report Errors: How to Dispute Errors on Your Report*. http://www.myfico.com/CreditEducation/Rights/FixingAnError.aspx (accessed July 3, 2014).

"How Credit Report Mistakes Are Made." *My Credit Report Is Wrong: Common Mistakes That Cause Report Errors*. http://www.myfico.com/CreditEducation/MistakesMade.aspx (accessed July 3, 2014).

"How Credit Scoring Helps Me." *Credit Scoring: How Credit Scores Help Consumers*. http://www.myfico.com/CreditEducation/ScoringHelps.aspx (accessed July 3, 2014).

"How to Repair My Credit and Improve My FICO Credit Score." *Improve Credit Score: Tips to Fix Poor Credit & Raise Your FICO Score*. http://www.myfico.com/CreditEducation/ImproveYourScore.aspx (accessed July 3, 2014).

"Identity theft." *Identity Theft: How to Help Protect Yourself & Signs to Watch For*. http://www.myfico.com/CreditEducation/IDTheft.aspx (accessed July 3, 2014).

"Missing Accounts on My Credit Report." *Credit Bureau Investigation*. http://www.myfico.com/CreditEducation/Rights/MissingAccount.aspx (accessed July 3, 2014).

"What's in My Credit Report?" *What's in Your Credit Report? Information That's in Every Report*. http://www.myfico.com/crediteducation/in-your-credit-report.aspx (accessed July 3, 2014).

"What's in My FICO Score." *FICO Credit Score Chart: How Credit Scores Are Calculated*. http://www.myfico.com/CreditEducation/WhatsInYourScore.aspx (accessed July 3, 2014).

"What's Not in My FICO Score." *Will This Affect My Credit Score? Find out What's NOT Included*. http://www.myfico.com/CreditEducation/WhatsNotInYourScore.aspx (accessed July 3, 2014).

Index

About the Author

SHINDY CHEN is an editorial manager at Vantage Production, a publisher of content and marketing materials and communications for mortgage industry professionals, their clients, and business referral partners. In this role she conceptualizes and creates digital and print content used for marketing and sales purposes.

Previously she was a vice president and regional mortgage manager at Wachovia Mortgage, now Wells Fargo Mortgage, and a senior loan originator at CTX Mortgage, sister company of former Fortune 250 home builder Centex Homes. Over her career she worked with more than 300 clients and their credit reports daily, closing over $100 million in gross mortgage volume.

Shindy worked in financial broadcast news at CNBC in the United States on the primetime show *Mad Money* with Jim Cramer and on European markets morning shows for Bloomberg TV in London, United Kingdom.

In addition to her current role she founded and curates Girl, Goin' Gone (www.girlgoingone.com), a female travel safety site.

Shindy also writes creative content and copy for tech start-ups and digital advertising agencies. Her work can be seen on websites, and web and mobile applications serving the entertainment, beauty, fashion, finance, and technology industries.

Shindy attended the University of North Carolina at Chapel Hill with a degree in English Literature, has an MBA from Georgia State University, and a Master de Management from the Sorbonne Graduate School of Business in Paris, France. She also studied at COPPEAD, the business school at Universidade Federal do Rio de Janeiro in Brazil.